D1364802

The Federal Government

INDEPENDENT GOVERNMENT AGENCIES

Working for America

Stephanie Buckwalter

MyReportLinks.com Books

an imprint of

 Enslow Publishers, Inc.

Box 398, 40 Industrial Road
Berkeley Heights, NJ 07922
USA

MyReportLinks.com Books, an imprint of Enslow Publishers, Inc. MyReportLinks®
is a registered trademark of Enslow Publishers, Inc.

Copyright © 2008 by Enslow Publishers, Inc.

All rights reserved.

No part of this book may be reproduced by any means
without the written permission of the publisher.

Library of Congress Cataloging-in-Publication Data

Buckwalter, Stephanie.
  Independent government agencies : working for America / Stephanie Buckwalter.
    p. cm. — (The federal government)
  Includes bibliographical references and index.
  ISBN-13: 978-1-59845-057-6
  ISBN-10: 1-59845-057-3
  1. Administrative agencies—United States—Juvenile literature. I. Title.
JK421.B798 2008
352.2'640973—dc22

                              2006023976

Printed in the United States of America

10 9 8 7 6 5 4 3 2 1

To Our Readers:
Through the purchase of this book, you and your library gain access to the Report Links that specifically back up this book.

The Publisher will provide access to the Report Links that back up this book and will keep these Report Links up to date on **www.myreportlinks.com** for five years from the book's first publication date.

We have done our best to make sure all Internet addresses in this book were active and appropriate when we went to press. However, the author and the Publisher have no control over, and assume no liability for, the material available on those Internet sites or on other Web sites they may link to.

The usage of the MyReportLinks.com Books Web site is subject to the terms and conditions stated on the Usage Policy Statement on **www.myreportlinks.com.**

A password may be required to access the Report Links that back up this book. The password is found on the bottom of page 4 of this book.

Any comments or suggestions can be sent by e-mail to comments@myreportlinks.com or to the address on the back cover.

♻ Enslow Publishers, Inc., is committed to printing our books on recycled paper. The paper in every book contains 10% to 30% post-consumer waste (PCW). The cover board on the outside of each book contains 100% PCW. Our goal is to do our part to help young people and the environment too!

Photo Credits: AmeriCorps, p. 3; Amtrak, p. 97; CIA, pp. 22, 24; CNCS photo by M. T. Harmon, Office of Public Affairs, p. 75; Corporation for National and Community Service, p. 74; Courtesy of Portraits of American History, © 1967 Dover Publications, Inc., p. 83; EEOC, p. 18; Enslow Publishers, Inc., p. 16; EPA, p. 10; *EXXON VALDEZ* Oil Spill Trustee Council, p. 8; Farm Credit Administration, p. 64; Federal Communications Commission, p. 95; Federal Deposit Insurance Corporation, p. 62; Federal Election Commission, p. 81; Federal Reserve Board, USA, p. 60; Library of Congress, pp. 46 (inset), 70, 78–79, 89; LSU Libraries, p. 19; MyReportLinks.com Books, p. 4; NARA, p. 91; NASA, pp. 1, 106–107, 108–109, 111; National Council on Disability, p. 72; National Endowment for the Arts, p. 114; National Labor Relations Board, p. 44; National Transportation Safety Board, p. 32; OSHA, p. 28; Overseas Private Investment Corporation, p. 42; Peace Corps, p. 116; Selective Service System, p. 87; Shutterstock.com, pp. 7, 33, 36, 46 (background), 48–49, 54–55, 93; Tom Pich/National Endowment for the Arts, p. 113; USA.gov, p. 85; USAID, p. 118; USCG/U.S. Dept. of Homeland Security, p. 12; U.S. Consumer Products Safety Commission, p. 30; U.S. Department of Defense, p. 58; U.S. Nuclear Regulatory Commission, p. 26; USPS, pp. 99, 101, 102; U.S. Securities and Exchange Commission, p. 56; U.S. Small Business Administration, p. 38; U.S. Social Security Administration, p. 66; U.S. Trade and Development Agency, p. 40.

Cover Photo: NASA

Contents

AmeriCorps volunteers ▷

MyReportLinks.com Books
Great Books, Great Links, Great for Research!

The Internet sites featured in this book can save you hours of research time. These Internet sites—we call them **"Report Links"**—are constantly changing, but we keep them up to date on our Web site.

When you see this "Approved Web Site" logo, you will know that we are directing you to a great Internet site that will help you with your research.

Give it a try! Type http://www.myreportlinks.com into your browser, click on the series title and enter the password, then click on the book title, and scroll down to the Report Links listed for this book.

The Report Links will bring you to great source documents, photographs, and illustrations. MyReportLinks.com Books save you time, feature Report Links that are kept up to date, and make report writing easier than ever! A complete listing of the Report Links can be found on pages 120–121 at the back of the book.

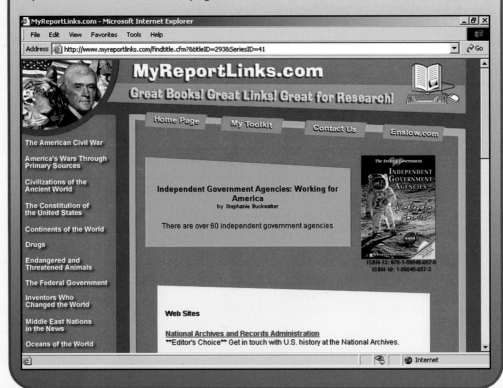

Please see "To Our Readers" on the copyright page for important information about this book, the MyReportLinks.com Web site, and the Report Links that back up this book.

Please enter IGA1229 if asked for a password.

Independent Government Agencies*

A

African Development
Foundation (ADF)
AMTRAK (National Railroad
Passenger Corporation)

C

Central Intelligence
Agency (CIA)
Commission on Civil Rights
Commodity Futures Trading
Commission (CFTC)
Consumer Product Safety
Commission (CPSC)
Corporation for National
and Community Service
Court Services and Offender
Supervision Agency
(CSOSA) for the District
of Columbia

D

Defense Nuclear Facilities
Safety Board (DNFSB)

E

Election Assistance
Commission (EAC)
Environmental Protection
Agency (EPA)
Equal Employment
Opportunity Commission
(EEOC)
Export-Import Bank of the
United States

F

Farm Credit Administration
(FCA)
Federal Communications
Commission (FCC)
Federal Deposit Insurance
Corporation (FDIC)
Federal Election
Commission (FEC)
Federal Housing
Finance Board
Federal Labor Relations
Authority
Federal Maritime
Commission
Federal Mediation and
Conciliation Service
Federal Mine Safety and
Health Review
Commission (FMSHC)
Federal Reserve System
Federal Retirement Thrift
Investment Board
Federal Trade
Commission (FTC)

G

General Services
Administration (GSA)

I

Institute of Museum and
Library Services
Inter-American Foundation
International Broadcasting
Bureau (IBB)

Independent Government Agencies*

M

Merit Systems Protection Board

N

National Aeronautics and Space Administration (NASA)

National Archives and Records Administration (NARA)

National Capital Planning Commission

National Council on Disability (NCD)

National Credit Union Administration (NCUA)

National Endowment for the Arts (NEA)

National Endowment for the Humanities (NEH)

National Labor Relations Board (NLRB)

National Mediation Board

National Science Foundation (NSF)

National Transportation Safety Board (NTSB)

Nuclear Regulatory Commission (NRC)

O

Occupational Safety and Health Review Commission (OSHRC)

Office of Compliance

Office of Government Ethics

Office of Personnel Management (OPM)

Office of Special Counsel (OSC)

Office of the National Counterintelligence Executive (ONCIX)

Overseas Private Investment Corporation

P

Panama Canal Commission

Peace Corps

Pension Benefit Guaranty Corporation (PBGC)

Postal Rate Commission

R

Railroad Retirement Board

Securities and Exchange Commission (SEC)

S

Selective Service System

Small Business Administration (SBA)

Social Security Administration (SSA)

T

Tennessee Valley Authority

U

U.S. Trade and Development Agency (USTDA)

United States Agency for International Development (USAID)

United States International Trade Commission (USITC)

United States Postal Service (USPS)

*Complete list as found on USA.gov

THE EPA CALLED INTO ACTION

1

Captain Joseph Hazelwood radioed the United States Coast Guard, "[We've] fetched up hard aground."[1] The *Exxon Valdez,* an oil tanker, had just run aground on Bligh Reef in Prince William Sound, Alaska. Captain Hazelwood mentioned the tanker was "evidently leaking some oil."[2] In fact, eight of its thirteen tanks were punctured when the tanker hit on the rocks. Eleven million gallons of crude oil gushed out into the water.

This oil spill on March 24, 1989, was the largest oil spill the United States had ever faced. The shoreline was covered in thick, slimy oil. Plants died from lack of oxygen. Birds sat grounded with wings too heavy to lift and too dirty to fly. Fishermen lost their livelihoods overnight as miles of oil covered their fishing grounds.

⇒CLEANUP

Responsibility for the cleanup operation ultimately fell to the United States Coast Guard. Other federal agencies arrived to help with the

▲ These workers are helping cleanse the soiled coastline that was the result of the Exxon Valdez oil spill. EPA employees spearheaded the cleanup effort.

massive effort. Clean up activities were delayed because of the remote location of the spill. Most areas were accessible by helicopter or boat only. At risk was the local commercial fishing industry, plus thousands of birds, waterfowl, sea otters, sea lions, and whales.

The Environmental Protection Agency (EPA) sent in its teams of engineers, scientists, and environmental protection specialists. The EPA helped with the application of chemical dispersants. The initial treatments did not break down the oil as expected. The Coast Guard decided there was not enough ocean wave action to mix the oil and the dispersants, so the effort was stopped.

Two other efforts to clean the oil off the water fell short. Isolating sections of the oil and then lighting it on fire did not work because of bad weather. They also tried to skim the oil off the water with special equipment. But there were many problems with the operation that slowed it down to the point that it was ineffective.

Although shoreline cleanup enjoyed a rapid start-up, wildlife rescue was slow. The remote location was part of the problem. Resources for rescue did not reach the scene soon enough. Many animals died from either loss of their food supply or direct contact with the oil. Government scientists estimated that as many as 250 bald eagles and 300,000 seabirds died.[3]

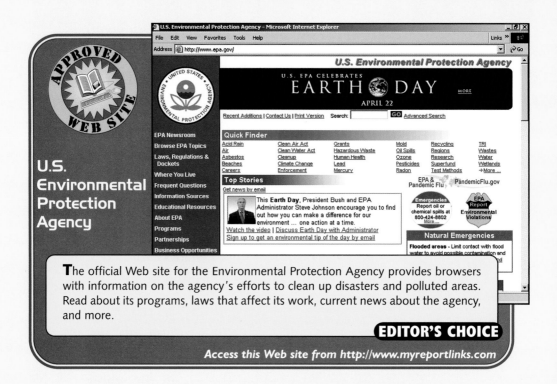

The official Web site for the Environmental Protection Agency provides browsers with information on the agency's efforts to clean up disasters and polluted areas. Read about its programs, laws that affect its work, current news about the agency, and more.

EDITOR'S CHOICE

Access this Web site from http://www.myreportlinks.com

→ RESCUING BIRDS

Once the wildlife rescue teams arrived, they moved into action. They immediately began capturing birds and taking them to treatment centers for medical aid and cleaning. The cleaning procedure follows a series of careful steps. First, oil is flushed from the eyes and intestines. Any thick patches of oil are wiped from the bird. The bird receives a high-level medical exam to check for injury. If needed, stomach-coating medicine can be used to prevent the intestines from absorbing any more oil.

If the bird cannot eat on its own, it is force-fed until it learns to feed itself. Once the bird responds well to its environment, workers use detergent to remove the oil from its feathers. A bird may require three or more washings to completely remove the oil.

Once the bird acts normally and is healthy, it is allowed to swim. The bird then takes over for the last stage of recovery. It begins to preen, or groom itself and get its feathers back into form for water survival. Once the bird demonstrates that it can float on the water and that its feathers do not absorb water, it is released. The cost of saving bald eagles averaged out to ten thousand dollars per bird saved.[4]

AFTERMATH

Today, the environment in Prince William Sound has healed itself. In fact, most of the long-lasting damage occurred from the cleanup measures. For example, hot water sprayed into tide pools got rid of the oil but it also killed all the life at the bottom of the food chain. Recovery there has been slow.

The Oil Pollution Act of 1990 required the Coast Guard to strengthen its regulations on oil tank vessels, owners, and operators. Oil tankers are now built with stronger hulls to keep similar oil spills from happening again. Emergency response supplies have been updated and put in strategic places.

The **United States Coast Guard** embarks on many missions for safety, national defense and security, and the protection of natural resources. Its official Web site also covers Coast Guard history, people, and vehicles. The Coast Guard works directly with many independent agencies.

→THE ENVIRONMENTAL PROTECTION AGENCY TODAY

Almost fourteen thousand oil spills are reported each year in the United States. The law requires that the responsible party report all spills to the federal government. The responsible group immediately cleans up most spills. However, some require assistance from local, state, or federal agencies.

The United States Coast Guard takes the lead on spills in coastal waters. The EPA is the lead federal response agency for oil spills in inland waters, such as bays, lakes, and rivers. The EPA also tracks all reports of oil spills. All are recorded in the Emergency Response Notification System (ERNS). ERNS has collected and maintained information on oil spills for the entire country since 1986. Future emergency response teams can access detailed information about how previous oil spills were handled.

2 WHAT IS AN INDEPENDENT GOVERNMENT AGENCY?

Do you wear a helmet when you ride your bicycle or skateboard? Have you ever flown in an airplane? Have you used the *World Factbook* to find information about a foreign country? If so, your life has been touched by an independent government agency.

Most of the independent government agencies are part of the executive branch. There are many, but each of the well-known ones will be covered in this book.

⮕WHERE DO THEY COME FROM?

Congress creates some independent government agencies through statutes. Statutes are simply laws passed by a legislative body. The president creates other agencies by executive order. Almost all independent government agencies are part of the executive branch of the United States government. Within each independent agency, there can be a miniature federal government structure. This means that these agencies can make rules (like the legislative branch), enforce them (like the executive branch), and review complaints (like the judicial branch).

Independent government agencies handle a particular part of our country's day-to-day operations. Statutes limit each agency's scope and authority, meaning an agency only has as much power as the statutes give it. For example, the National Aeronautics and Space Administration (NASA) can only make rules that apply to spaceflight. The Equal Employment Opportunity Commission (EEOC) can only make rules that apply to hiring employees.

⊜ HOW ARE THEY MONITORED?

The president usually appoints the heads of the independent agencies, but the president does not directly control the agencies. Some report to him, but most report to the various departments in the president's cabinet.

The Administrative Procedure Act of 1946 created procedures for how agencies can function.

THE EXECUTIVE BRANCH

PRESIDENT

VICE PRESIDENT

OFFICE OF THE VICE PRESIDENT

EXECUTIVE DEPARTMENTS

- Department of Agriculture
- Department of Commerce
- Department of Defense
- Department of Education
- Department of Energy
- Department of Health and Human Services
- Department of Homeland Security

- Department of Housing and Urban Development
- Department of Interior
- Department of Justice
- Department of Labor
- Department of State
- Department of Transportation
- Department of the Treasury
- Department of Verterans Affairs

INDEPENDENT AGENCIES
see list on pp. 5–6

▲ The structure of the Executive Branch of the U.S. federal government.
Most independent agencies are overseen by the president or the heads of
the executive departments.

Lawsuits related to any independent agency are handled in the District of Columbia. They are filed in the D.C. Circuit Court. The lawsuit can then be appealed to the United States Supreme Court.

⊖ARE THERE DIFFERENT TYPES OF INDEPENDENT GOVERNMENT AGENCIES?

The federal government has a vocabulary all its own. Many of the independent agency names and purposes include words that may be new to you. Here are some terms that will help you navigate the world of government agencies.

The first group of terms defines how the agency is organized:

- An **agency** is an organization or department that is given permission to act for someone else. Independent government agencies act on behalf of the government.

- A **commission** is a group or organization given authority to carry out the wishes of another.

- A **board** is a group of leaders, usually five members in the case of independent government agencies, who review how the agency operates and then recommend changes.

Then there are terms that describe what an agency does. A government agency can regulate, mediate, adjudicate, or review.

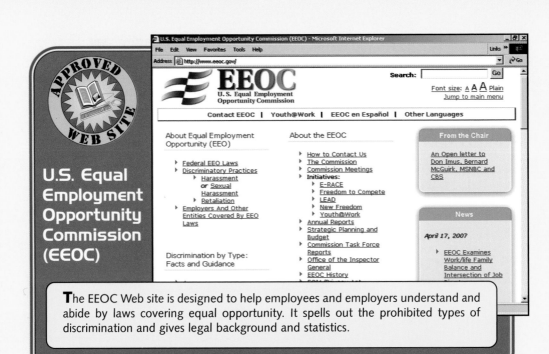

The EEOC Web site is designed to help employees and employers understand and abide by laws covering equal opportunity. It spells out the prohibited types of discrimination and gives legal background and statistics.

Access this Web site from http://www.myreportlinks.com

- To **regulate** means to govern according to rules. An agency with regulatory authority makes and enforces rules.

- To **mediate** means to come between two or more parties to help them solve a problem. When mediation is sought, the parties agree to accept whatever decision the mediator makes.

- To **adjudicate** means to judge evidence and decide who is right and who is wrong, as in a trial. Independent government agencies that adjudicate usually have the power to give out penalties, too.

Still other independent government agencies work to provide an impartial view of government processes or actions. These agencies might work as mediators, adjudicators, or advisors to Congress or the president. The members of these agencies keep an open mind and work to ensure that all events and trials are handled fairly.

The current list of independent government agencies falls into seven basic groups. These groups are based on overall purpose rather than the function each performs. The groups are:

- Safety and Security
- Commerce and Business
- Financial

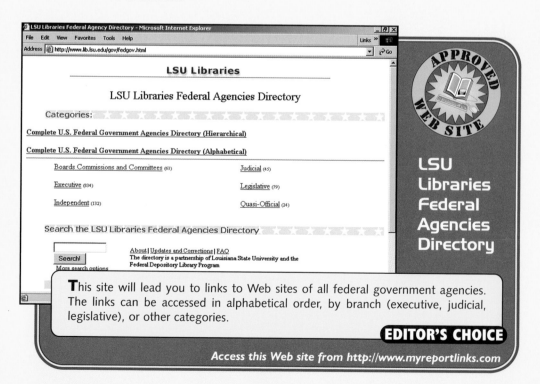

This site will lead you to links to Web sites of all federal government agencies. The links can be accessed in alphabetical order, by branch (executive, judicial, legislative), or other categories.

EDITOR'S CHOICE

Access this Web site from http://www.myreportlinks.com

- •Citizen Support
- •Government Support
- •Travel and Communication
- •Science, the Arts, and Humanity

Regardless of purpose, all independent government agencies work to support the federal government in the interest of the people.

SAFETY AND SECURITY

3

One group of the many independent government agencies has a major impact on a citizen's everyday life. The Central Intelligence Agency (CIA) and the Office of the National Counterintelligence Executive (ONCIX) work to protect the United States from outside threats. The other agencies in this chapter work to keep Americans safe as they work, play, stay at home, and travel.

➔SECURITY

Double agents, spies, and lies. Is this what comes to mind when you hear CIA? The CIA is part of the executive branch of the government. Covert, or undercover, operations are carried out at the direction of the president. But this is only one job of the CIA.

The CIA hires many other types of people such as scientists, engineers, economists, linguists, mathematicians, secretaries, accountants, and computer specialists, among others. These people collect data about foreign governments, corporations, and individuals. Once this data is analyzed,

▲ CIA headquarters is located in Langley, Virginia. Many of the things that occur there are top-secret and the highest-level security clearance is needed to get far once you are inside.

it is called intelligence. Intelligence is arranged into reports. These reports go to our nation's decision makers. Some reports are offered to the public in printed form or in the CIA's Electronic Reading Room.

One such report from the CIA is the *World Fact-book*. This book lists countries all over the world. It provides information on each country's government structure, the makeup of the population, called demographics, and various statistics. The CIA publishes the book online and in printed book form.

⇒CIA HISTORY

The CIA was formed in 1947 for a specific purpose. Just after World War II ended, the United States entered into a Cold War with the Union of Soviet Socialist Republics (USSR). Americans at that time commonly referred to the USSR as "Russia," but Russia was only one country in the USSR. This Cold War was not a military battle, but a standoff between the world's two superpowers. Each had developed a nuclear program that could wipe out the other country. Each country lived under the constant threat of nuclear war.

The original vision for the CIA was to create a group within the United States government that could match the USSR's KGB spy force. The USSR was closed to most outsiders, so the United States

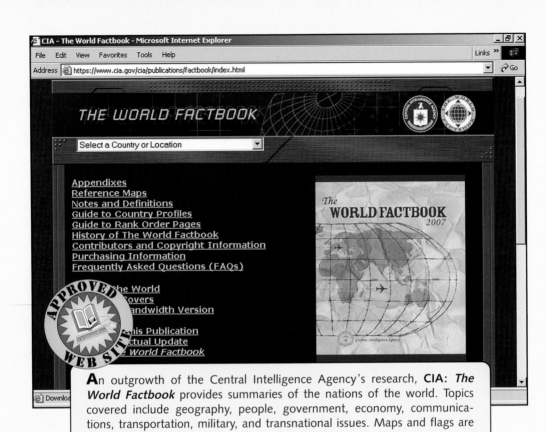

CIA - The World Factbook - Microsoft Internet Explorer

File   Edit   View   Favorites   Tools   Help   Links »

Address https://www.cia.gov/cia/publications/factbook/index.html   Go

THE WORLD FACTBOOK

Select a Country or Location

Appendixes
Reference Maps
Notes and Definitions
Guide to Country Profiles
Guide to Rank Order Pages
History of The World Factbook
Contributors and Copyright Information
Purchasing Information
Frequently Asked Questions (FAQs)

The
WORLD FACTBOOK
2007

An outgrowth of the Central Intelligence Agency's research, **CIA:** *The World Factbook* provides summaries of the nations of the world. Topics covered include geography, people, government, economy, communications, transportation, military, and transnational issues. Maps and flags are included, too.

relied on spies to get information on the USSR's military development and plans.

With the fall of the Berlin Wall in 1989, the Cold War ended. Terrorism is now the major international threat. Unlike enemies in traditional wars of the past, terrorists are not tied to just one country. They can have members spread across several countries. The CIA has changed to meet these new challenges. It now falls under the direction of the United States Intelligence Community, a group of sixteen agencies that work separately and together to fight threats from terrorists and other enemies of the United States.

The United States government also has a counterintelligence agency, headed by the National Counterintelligence Executive (NCIX). Counter intelligence means to counter, or respond to, any intelligence activities of one country directed against another country. Just as the United States gathers intelligence, so do other countries and enemy groups. They seek to break down our national security, crack open our security systems, spread false information to wrongly influence our own intelligence efforts, and acquire technology and weapons to harm the United States.

The Office of the National Counterintelligence Executive takes a close look at threats from these entities and responds to them. When a foreign intelligence operation is identified, the NCIX works proactively to break up its intelligence network. It also spreads false information to confound our enemies. The NCIX works with the United States Intelligence Community to share information and support existing intelligence efforts.

➔ SAFETY IN NUCLEAR DEVELOPMENT

There are about 140 nuclear reactors in the United States. A nuclear reactor produces energy by splitting atoms. Some nuclear reactors are used by the military to make weapons, others are used

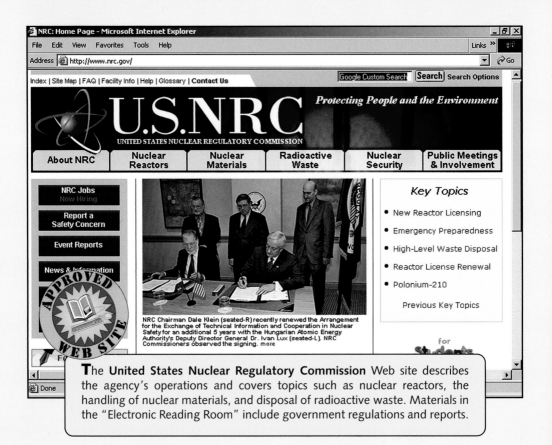

NRC: Home Page - Microsoft Internet Explorer

File   Edit   View   Favorites   Tools   Help   Links »

Address   http://www.nrc.gov/   Go

Index | Site Map | FAQ | Facility Info | Help | Glossary | **Contact Us**   Google Custom Search [Search] Search Options

U.S.NRC
UNITED STATES NUCLEAR REGULATORY COMMISSION   *Protecting People and the Environment*

| About NRC | Nuclear Reactors | Nuclear Materials | Radioactive Waste | Nuclear Security | Public Meetings & Involvement |

NRC Jobs
Now Hiring

Report a
Safety Concern

Event Reports

News & Information

Key Topics

• New Reactor Licensing

• Emergency Preparedness

• High-Level Waste Disposal

• Reactor License Renewal

• Polonium-210

   Previous Key Topics

NRC Chairman Dale Klein (seated-R) recently renewed the Arrangement
for the Exchange of Technical Information and Cooperation in Nuclear
Safety for an additional 5 years with the Hungarian Atomic Energy
Authority's Deputy Director General Dr. Ivan Lux (seated-L). NRC
Commissioners observed the signing. more

for
Students

Done

The **United States Nuclear Regulatory Commission** Web site describes the agency's operations and covers topics such as nuclear reactors, the handling of nuclear materials, and disposal of radioactive waste. Materials in the "Electronic Reading Room" include government regulations and reports.

by civilians to generate nuclear power. Nuclear production creates radioactive materials. These materials are harmful to humans, animals, and the environment.

There are two independent government agencies concerned with nuclear production. The one you might hear about on the evening news is the Nuclear Regulatory Commission. It regulates the nation's civilian use of nuclear power including medicine, power, and university research. It works to protect both people and the environment from the effects of radiation.

The United States maintains an arsenal of nuclear weapons as well. Some of the jobs related to the storage of nuclear weapons include dismantling surplus weapons, disposing of radioactive materials, cleaning up radioactive waste, and building new facilities. The Defense Nuclear Facilities Safety Board oversees the military use of nuclear products. Run by the Department of Energy, it is designed to protect the public, workers, and the environment from everyday hazards and accidents.

➲ SAFETY AT WORK

The Department of Labor has a major influence on the workplace and how it is run. Some of its agencies set health and safety standards for the workplace. Two such agencies are the Occupational Safety and Health Review Administration (OSHA) and the Mine Safety and Health Administration (MSHA). These agencies enforce the standards set by the Department of Labor. They send inspectors to visit the workplace. When a company does not follow the rules, the inspectors can write citations and assess penalties.

But what happens when the business or agency that is written up for breaking a rule disagrees? Both OSHA and MSHA have related independent government agencies to solve disputes between the agency and the employer. OSHA works with

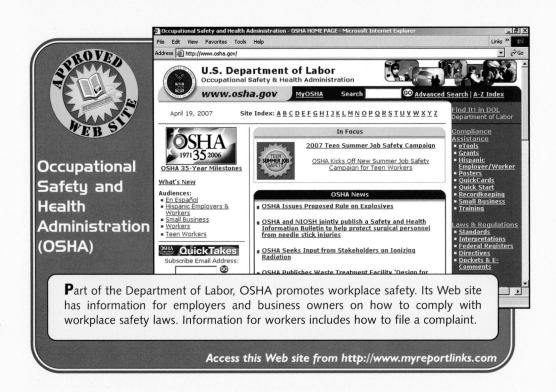

Occupational
Safety and
Health
Administration
(OSHA)

Part of the Department of Labor, OSHA promotes workplace safety. Its Web site has information for employers and business owners on how to comply with workplace safety laws. Information for workers includes how to file a complaint.

Access this Web site from http://www.myreportlinks.com

the Occupational Safety and Health Review Commission (OSHRC) and MSHA works with the Federal Mine Safety and Health Review Commission. The sole purpose of these agencies is to resolve disputes. They function as a court that can conduct hearings, receive evidence, and hand down decisions, including penalties.

⊖SAFETY OF THE ENVIRONMENT

The emergency response of the Environmental Protection Agency was highlighted in Chapter One. The normal routine of the EPA does not usually include massive environmental rescues.

Rather, it involves dealing with the slow, daily buildup of toxins that can pollute the nation's water, land, and air. Since it was formed in 1970, the EPA has taken on countless tasks. It regulates some of the things that affect us every day. The EPA sets air quality and safe drinking water standards. It regulates disposal of toxic substances so they do not poison our water supply or cause sickness. It also works for the benefit of endangered species, protecting their natural habitats in order to give them a chance to thrive again.

SAFETY AT HOME

The EPA responds to environmental problems. The Consumer Product Safety Commission (CPSC) responds to another type of problem. These problems involve goods sold to the American people.

Almost everything you use from the time you are born until the time you die is regulated by this agency. The crib you slept in, the toys you played with, and the bicycle helmet you wear now. The CPSC influences how cell phones, heaters, and high chairs are made.

The CPSC was formed in 1972. Its purpose is to protect the public "from unreasonable risks of serious injury or death from more than fifteen thousand types of consumer products under the agency's jurisdiction."[1] It regulates the sale and manufacture of most consumer goods offered in

U.S.
Consumer
Product
Safety
Commission

The CPSC is devoted to preventing injury that can result from unsafe products. Its Web site describes current and historical product recalls, gives information on voluntary safety guidelines, has information for business owners and manufacturers, and even has podcasts on safety recalls.

Access this Web site from http://www.myreportlinks.com

the United States. The only exceptions are those items covered by other agencies. The CPSC does not regulate anything covered by the Food and Drug Administration (FDA), the National Highway Traffic Safety Administration (NHTSA), and the Bureau of Alcohol, Tobacco, Firearms and Explosives (ATF).

What about when something goes wrong with a product? Product problems can affect millions of people. The problem might be so severe that it causes death. Or it might not even be a problem yet, just a potential problem. When either of these is brought to the CPSC's attention, the CPSC requires the manufacturer to solve the problem. The maker must recall the product, or request that it be sent back to them, to either fix or replace it. A recall is expensive, so most companies make their products safe to begin with.

The CPSC must have the ability to spread the news about a recall widely and quickly. Product recalls must be issued and posted in as many places as possible for the consumer to find out about them. Some of the most common ways of getting the word out are by posting information online, producing posters, sending out press releases, and by broadcasting paid advertisements.

➔TRANSPORTATION SAFETY

The National Transportation Safety Board (NTSB) investigates every civil aviation accident to determine the probable cause. Civil aviation accidents are those that involve nonmilitary aircraft. The NTSB is an independent agency, that works closely with the Federal Aviation Administration (FAA) and U.S. Department of Transportation.

The board is made up of five members. They send out teams to develop factual records of what occurred and then make safety recommendations based on what the teams find. Because the NTSB has developed a solid reputation for thoroughness

The NTSB's motto is "Safety is Our Destination." Its Web site has sections on traffic safety, vehicles and equipment, research, and laws and regulations. Examples of what is covered on the site include details of its safety campaigns, crash test results, and summaries of relevant laws and regulations.

Access this Web site from http://www.myreportlinks.com

and fairness, 82 percent of their recommendations are accepted.

Aviation accidents make up most of the investigations. However, the NTSB investigates other transportation accidents, too. These accidents involve highways, marine craft, pipelines, and railways. They always get called in if the accident involves the release of hazardous materials. These accidents, called surface accidents, involve much smaller teams of experts.

The NTSB investigates about two thousand aviation accidents and five hundred other transportation accidents a year. Once an accident is reported, the NTSB sends out a Go Team. The purpose of the Go Team is to get to the site as quickly as possible. Then the team gathers just the right experts to study the accident. These experts might come from one of many areas.

The Go Team reports to the Investigator-in-Charge (IIC) who runs the investigation. Each Go Team member becomes head of its subgroup. Each subgroup includes experts and other parties who

▲ *The NTSB works with local officials and the Federal Aviation Administration to help investigate transportation accidents. These men are helping out at the scene of a plane crash.*

might have helpful information. Other parties might include people from the Federal Aviation Administration, pilots and flight attendants unions, airplane manufacturers, and so on. The flight data and cockpit voice recorder teams meet at NTSB's headquarters in Washington, D.C.

While the investigators work on the scene, one of the board members is present and speaks to the press. He or she briefs the media, informing them only of factual information gathered so far.

Once the on-site investigation is complete, the work groups move on to finish their research. Some may go to airplane factories, pilot-training facilities, or to the NTSB headquarters. Once analysis is complete, a draft report is sent to the board. The board reviews the report and finalizes it. The board publishes parts of the report, called an abstract. This summary contains the board's conclusions, the probable cause of the accident, and any safety recommendations.

COMMERCE AND BUSINESS

4

Our economy depends on consumer spending and businesses growing. It is in the best interest of the government to keep the economy healthy, and the businesses that drive that economy healthy too. Therefore, several independent government agencies help promote and protect the day-to-day operations of businesses in the United States.

→PROTECTING TRADE

The United States has a free market economy. This means that the economy is based on what consumers want and are willing to purchase. It also assumes that business deals are done honestly. In a free market economy, the government only

35

△ There are a handful of independent agencies whose members' main concern is helping to foster a healthy economy. One of these is the Small Business Administration which, among other things, approves loans to small businesses.

intervenes in the market processes when necessary to keep this system working. This is what makes it free—it is free from outside intervention.

Over time, the government has stepped in to help businesses start up, to keep the competition fair, and to limit interference from overseas interests. There are four independent government agencies to protect businesses from unfair trade practices. A quick trip to José's Hermie Hut will highlight some of the services of each one as José sets up his business selling land hermit crabs.[1]

⮕SETTING UP A SMALL BUSINESS

After all his research, José decides that the best place to set up his hermit crab business is at a kiosk, or small stand, in the mall. Start-up costs and rent will be more than he can afford, so he goes to the Small Business Administration (SBA) for help. The SBA offers him advice on creating a business plan, helps him figure out which licenses he will need, and provides access to a local Small Business Development Center. José finds out that the SBA does not lend money directly to businesses. Instead, it works with the lenders who loan the money. The SBA will guarantee the loan of a small business so if the borrower cannot pay back the loan, the SBA will pay off the loan for the borrower. With his business plan in hand, José goes to a lender. The bank is a little hesitant, but after the loan officer gets a guarantee from the SBA, José gets his loan. He is ready to roll.

Next, José picks a supplier for the crabs. Land hermit crabs live in tropical environments, so he has to order them from places near the Caribbean Sea. He checks with the Federal Maritime Commission to see if his supplier, Slick Eddy's Imports, has the proper license for importing hermit crabs.

http://www.sba.gov/ - Microsoft Internet Explorer

File   Edit   View   Favorites   Tools   Help   Links »

Address http://www.sba.gov/   Go

U.S. Small Business Administration

SBA
Your Small Business Resource

Programs and services to help
you start, grow and succeed

> En Español

Search SBA   GO

Home	SMALL BUSINESS PLANNER	SERVICES	TOOLS	LOCAL RESOURCES
About SBA				
Newsroom				
Contact				

Manage your business   Expand your business   Increase your business   Support your business
from start to finish   with programs and services knowledge and productivity   with a team of experts

SPOTLIGHT

SBA Success Story
Building a successful business
by exceeding Expectations -
Payal Tak journeyed from

Online Business Chat
"Ask the SBA"
April 30, 2007 at 1pm (ET)

Helping Americans establish, run, and expand their own businesses is the goal of the **U.S. Small Business Administration.** Its Web site has different "views" with tools and information for each stage of business development. The site also includes news stories, profiles, summaries of relevant laws and regulations, and links to other government agencies.

His supplier checks out as being a trustworthy operation, so José is ready to open for business.

Within a few weeks, business is booming. The word is out and his store becomes a favorite stop at the mall. Another month goes by and business begins to drop. José assumes it is because the novelty has worn off and people are just looking now. Then he finds out that the pet store across from the mall has begun using hermit crab sales as a tie-in to the purchase of snakes. This means that the pet store is requiring customers to purchase a hermit crab each time they buy a snake. Tie-ins are illegal when they harm the competition. José contacts the Federal Trade Commission (FTC) and reports the activity. The FTC visits the pet store and the problem is cleared up.

After about a year, José's customers tell him that their hermit crabs only live about six months to a year. José realizes that the typical plastic cases sold with hermit crabs are not designed to recreate the tropical environment of the crab's natural habitat. He designs a new carrier with a removable coconut fiber wall that can be dampened to help keep the plastic cages humidified. Then he applies for a patent, a process that can take up to five years. He is awarded both United States and international patents on the design. This official document states that no one can copy the model he created. He begins to sell more cages than hermit crabs.

JOSÉ GETS HELP

A few months later, sales of the cages drop off. José overhears a customer say, "Don't buy one of those here. They're much cheaper online at crabitatsforcheap.com."[2] José checks out the site and sees copies of his patented design for sale. He checks to see who runs the Web site. He finds out that his supplier, Slick Eddy—who visits

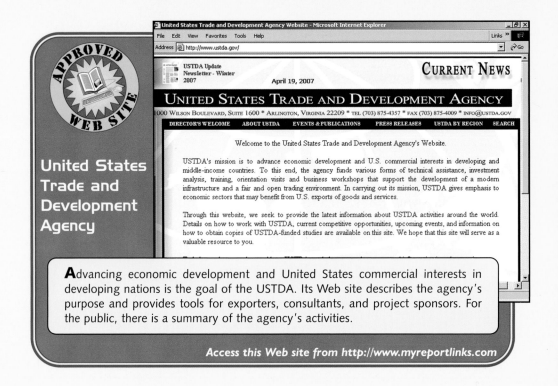

United States
Trade and
Development
Agency

Advancing economic development and United States commercial interests in developing nations is the goal of the USTDA. Its Web site describes the agency's purpose and provides tools for exporters, consultants, and project sponsors. For the public, there is a summary of the agency's activities.

Access this Web site from http://www.myreportlinks.com

periodically for customer service—has stolen his idea and is marketing it worldwide. José approaches the United States International Trade Commission to help him protect his international copyright. They investigate José's claim and take the necessary steps to protect his copyright. The investigation may take several years.

After these rocky first few years, José's business takes off and becomes a retail chain with kiosks in malls all across the United States. Although he has repaid his loans and no longer qualifies for help from the SBA, he probably never would have made it without their help.

→DEVELOPING TRADE ABROAD

In addition to protecting trade on United States soil, independent agencies also help U.S. investors and businesses develop trade overseas. The United States Trade and Development Agency (USTDA) works in two ways. The first is to help developing countries build an infrastructure that will support their economic goals. An infrastructure includes things like transportation, energy and power, water and the environment, health care, mining and natural resources, telecommunications, and information technology. To do this, the agency provides overseas grants, contracts with United States companies, and trust funds with bank groups.

The Trade and Development Agency also helps American businesses export their products and services. This export of goods creates jobs at home in the United States. The USTDA works with many other federal and independent agencies to accomplish their goals. These include the Departments of State, Commerce, Homeland Security, and Transportation; the Export-Import Bank of the United States; and the Overseas Private Investment Corporation.

The Overseas Private Investment Corporation is also an independent government agency. It helps United States businesses invest overseas to help with the economic and social development of

Overseas Private Investment Corporation - Microsoft Internet Explorer

File Edit View Favorites Tools Help

Links »

Address http://www.opic.gov/

Home · Subscribe to news · Site Map   Search   GO

Doing Business With Us   News & Events   Publications & Resources   About Us   Partners

FINANCING

INSURANCE

INVESTMENT FUNDS

An Agency of the United States Government

Small Bus

Supporting
U.S. Foreign Policy

Project Profile

Updates

> Investment Funds Call for Proposals -
  Africa Capital Markets

> OPIC Launches New Transparency Initiative

ACCESS TO OPPORTUNITY IN
CENTRAL AMERICA AND THE
CARIBBEAN
An International Investment Conference
Co-hosted by the Overseas Private Investment Corporation
MAY 15-17, 2007
San Salvador El Salvador
REGISTER TODAY

Done

Overseas Private Investment Corporation (OPIC) is an independent agency that supports investment in emerging markets to help the development and growth of free markets. Its Web site is geared primarily to investors and business owners in the United States. It features news and events, details on financing projects and insurance, and a project profile.

countries moving from a nonmarket economy to a market economy. The overall goals are to increase United States competitiveness in the international market, help less-developed nations expand their economies, and promote United States national and foreign policy interests.

➔LABOR RELATIONS

The formula for good business requires balancing the interests of the owners of a company (management) with the concerns of the employees (labor) and the needs of the customer. Some requirements on the owners' list would include things like making a profit, serving the customers' needs, and growing the company. An employee's requirements would include fair pay, a safe workplace, and rewards for hard work. The customers' needs might be a certain product, a certain level of service, or a certain price.

⊖LABOR AND MANAGEMENT

The United States government allows workers to organize into groups to make sure their needs are addressed. These groups bargain with management as one unit, sometimes called a union. The union has leaders who meet with management and resolve differences. The agreements made affect all workers who are members of that union.

At times, the needs of labor and management may be in conflict. It is not always possible for the parties involved to work things out on their own. The federal government has created several agencies to help keep companies running smoothly when conflicts arise.

The Federal Labor Relations Authority helps all federal employees, except those who work for the U.S. Postal Service. The authority:

- resolves complaints of unfair labor practices
- determines the appropriateness of units for labor organization representation

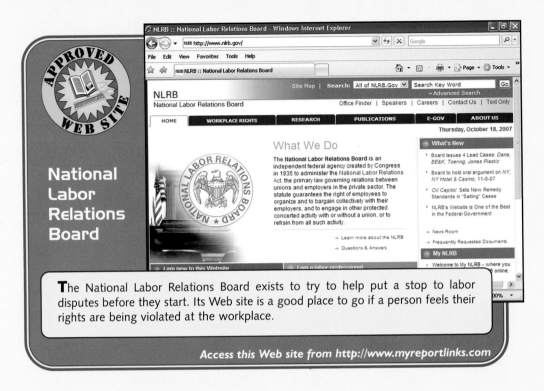

National
Labor
Relations
Board

The National Labor Relations Board exists to try to help put a stop to labor disputes before they start. Its Web site is a good place to go if a person feels their rights are being violated at the workplace.

Access this Web site from http://www.myreportlinks.com

- adjudicates exceptions to arbitrator's awards
- adjudicates legal issues relating to duty to bargain/negotiability
- resolves impasses during negotiations

The National Labor Relations Board works with unions and all employers in the private sector involved in interstate commerce, except airlines, railroads, agriculture, and government. The goal of the board is to maintain industrial peace.

The National Mediation Board serves as mediator between labor and management in the airline and railroad industries. Their main goal is to minimize work stoppages in these important transportation industries. The Federal Mediation and Conciliation Service provides mediation and conflict resolution services to industry, government agencies, and communities. This service is not restricted to those groups who have organized into bargaining units, or unions.

→ TENNESSEE VALLEY AUTHORITY

The Tennessee Valley is the area along the banks of the Tennessee River. It covers most of Tennessee, large portions of Alabama and Mississippi, plus small portions of four other states. After years of overuse and misuse by farmers and lumber companies, the land along this river was no longer productive. President Franklin Roosevelt had a bold solution, one that would eventually lead to the nation's largest public power company.

Roosevelt created a federally owned company called the Tennessee Valley Authority in 1933 to focus on energy, environment, and economic development of that area. Some parts of the project were considered a success, others were not. The initial approach to the problems in the Tennessee Valley was to look at each problem—and there were many—individually and as part of the whole project. This led to solutions that supported the goals of all three areas of improvement. This approach is still used today and allows the TVA to stay competitive in the changing utilities market. The utilities are companies that provide things like

The Fontana Dam, located in western North Carolina, was a major project of the TVA. Franklin D. Roosevelt (inset) created the TVA in 1933.

heat, electricity, and water service. TVA is the nation's largest public power company.

→PANAMA CANAL COMMISSION

The first explorers from Europe—Christopher Columbus, Amerigo Vespucci, Ferdinand Magellan— looked for it but could not find it. They searched the coasts of North and South America, knowing that the first to find it would make rich the country that paid for his trip. The only problem was that until 1906 it did not exist. There was no passable waterway connecting the Atlantic Ocean to the Pacific Ocean. The only way to sail from one side of the Americas to the other was to sail around Cape Horn at the southern tip of South America.

In 1880, the French began construction on a canal across the narrow strip of land known as the Isthmus of Panama. They abandoned the project in 1893, partly because of the difficulty in building the type of canal they wanted, but mostly because of the high number of workers who died from disease. In 1904, the United States picked up construction of the canal in exchange for control of the Panama Canal Zone and helping Panama gain its independence from Colombia. The canal, approximately forty-eight miles (seventy-seven kilometers) long, opened in 1914. Although a Northwest Passage through the Arctic Ocean had been found by this time, it was not until 1969 that

This image is from the view of a boat as it makes its way through the Gatun Locks of the Panama Canal.

it was useable. Meanwhile, the Panama Canal was, and continues to be, highly traveled.

The Panama Canal Commission was an agency that was jointly run by the United States and Panama. It managed the Panama Canal. On December 31, 1999, the United States gave up its claim on managing the canal. It is now managed by the Panama Canal Authority (ACP), an agency of the government of Panama. The ACP now has complete control over all management and administration of the canal. Even though it is no longer in operation, the Panama Canal Commission remains on the independent government agency Web site. Some Americans still serve on the ACP.

FINANCIAL

5

The United States is rich. It is rich in knowledge and skills, it is rich in humanitarian aid, and it is rich in dollars. Part of the reason for this wealth is the overall health of its economy. The federal government has created several agencies to promote and maintain this health.

First, a high-level view of the economy might be helpful. The United States has a consumer-driven economy. The market is driven by what people are willing to buy. The more people buy, the more money businesses make. The more they make, the more money they have to research and create new products and to expand their existing businesses. As businesses do well, they increase how much they pay their employees. As people make more money, they buy more products. And the cycle goes on.

The economy grows even more when people use credit. Credit is a promise to pay based on future income. Even though people are spending money they do not have yet, it is still spending.

When there is a break somewhere in this cycle, then the economy slows down or stops growing. It can even decline. Many of the independent government agencies were created to help make sure the economy continues to expand over time. Of these, eight are specifically concerned with the stock market, banking, and credit institutions. Another four were created to help protect people's retirement savings. Although the workings of the economy are complex, looking at these agencies will give you several pieces of the puzzle.

⇨THE STOCK MARKET

The New York Stock Exchange (NYSE) is the largest public stock market in the world. Images of the NYSE include the opening and closing bells, people yelling and gesturing to each other, and pieces of paper all over the floor. What you are seeing is a live public auction. To understand the workings of it, consider auctions on eBay. There are sellers and buyers. The sellers list their products and the item goes to the highest bidder—the person who has offered the most money for the product. EBay is not the buyer or the seller. It is the company that facilitates the exchange.

A stock market works the same way, except there is no end time. There are buyers and sellers of stock. Stock is sold to the highest bidder, but the price can go up or down based on market conditions. Therefore, there are no guarantees. An investor can make money in the stock market, but he or she can also lose it. The media reports on the daily ups and downs of the market, giving the market a sort of daily "end time."

Stocks are initially offered by a company in order to raise money, called capital. This initial offering of stock is called the primary market for stock. Once offered, the stock can be bought and sold many times. Investors buy and sell stock to make money as the prices change, leading to a secondary market. Both types of transactions are necessary for the operation of a stock market.

STOCK EXCHANGES

To make stock transactions fair, there is an underlying assumption that each potential investor has the same information to work from. The Securities and Exchange Commission (SEC) was created to oversee this whole process. All of the laws related to stock trading can be summed up in two ideas. First, companies offering stock must tell the

The Wall Street entrance to the New York Stock Exchange, New York City. Regulating the trade of stocks and bonds is the responsibility of independent agencies of the federal government.

The online home of the U.S. Securities and Exchange Commission tells of how the group monitors to ensure that the buying and selling of stocks is done fairly. Click on "What We Do" for more information.

Access this Web site from http://www.myreportlinks.com

public the truth about their businesses. Second, people who trade stocks, called securities, must treat investors fairly.

The NYSE is only one stock exchange. There is also the American Stock Exchange (AMEX), smaller regional exchanges, and the Nasdaq. The Nasdaq is unique in that all transactions are handled electronically. All other stock markets use human interaction in the buying and selling process. The SEC oversees all the American stock exchanges and all the people who deal with the buying and selling of stock.

Commodities futures are also traded on the market. Commodities are goods bought and sold.

Commodities futures are the prices a buyer of raw materials would expect to pay for a particular type of goods in the future. Examples of goods traditionally traded on the futures market are gold, oil, and farm products like grain, pork, and beef. More recently, the futures market has expanded to include foreign currencies and other financial instruments.

Stocks move relatively slowly over time because they are tied to the health of a particular company. Futures, on the other hand, can be volatile. They can change rapidly up or down in a single day. One world news event can drastically alter prices on the futures market. That is because futures depend on unpredictable things like weather for farm crops, political stability in the Middle East for oil, and the overall health of the global financial markets for gold.

Because of this volatility, there is a lot of potential for abuse of the system. The Commodity Futures Trading Commission was created to protect both market users and the public from abuses such as fraud and manipulation. It works closely with the SEC, the Federal Reserve, and the Treasury Department to protect the markets.

⇒ BANKING

Did you know that the United States has its own bank? The Federal Reserve System, often referred to as the Federal Reserve or simply "the Fed," is the central bank of the United States. The Fed maintains the stability of the nation's financial system with a goal of full employment and stable prices. The numbers you hear mentioned on the news include the unemployment rate and the interest rate. The unemployment rate indicates the percentage of the population that is out of work. The interest rate indicates how much it will

▲ A burning oil field in Iraq. Turmoil in other parts of the world can negatively affect the economy of the United States.

cost to borrow money. The Fed can raise or lower the interest rate in order to reduce or stimulate spending of both businesses and individuals.

Alan Greenspan served as chairman of the Federal Reserve for eighteen years, from 1988 to 2006. He served five presidents. He has been hailed by many as a guru of the financial markets. He was a master at controlling the interest rate to get a desired effect. During his tenure, he presided over the largest expansion of economic growth since World War II. He was known for being a fair team player, as evidenced by his challenge to a group of graduating college students: "The true measure of a career is to be able to be content, even proud, that you succeeded through your own endeavors without leaving a trail of casualties in your wake."[1] Just before retirement, he was awarded the Presidential Medal of Freedom, America's highest civilian award.

FDIC

The stock market crash of 1929 created a panic when the value of people's investments went from thousands of dollars to just pennies in a day. Many banks had taken people's deposits and invested heavily in the stock market. When the stock market crashed, the banks could not give people their money when they wanted to withdraw it. The banks basically had to close their doors because

▲ Greenspan (left) is shaking hands with Secretary of Defense Donald Rumsfeld after receiving a medal for public service. Alan Greenspan served as chairman of the Federal Reserve for almost two decades.

they had no money for people to withdraw. Many people lost not only their investment money, but also their everyday living expenses deposited in their banks.

In response to this disaster, the Federal Deposit Insurance Corporation (FDIC) was created. It insures people's deposits in participating financial institutions up to $100,000. Since the creation of the FDIC, not a single person has lost his or her money due to a bank failure.

⊝ CREDIT

After the stock market crash of 1929, the economy came to a halt. People started hoarding their money for fear of losing it. For almost a decade, there was no inflation, but there was also relatively little new spending. Around this time, the nation's financial institutions began to issue credit to their customers. This began a cycle of borrowing and spending that continues today.

Recall that credit is simply a promise to pay back a lender in the future. The modern era of lending was in its earliest stages after World War II. Lending was primarily used to purchase homes or businesses. These types of loans are considered investments because the value of these items tends to increase over time. These loans are relatively low-risk for the lender because if the borrower does not repay the loan, the lending

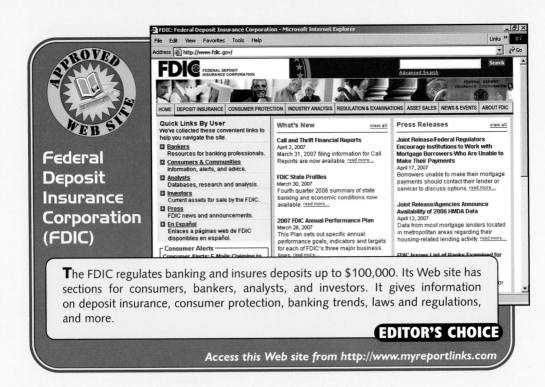

Federal
Deposit
Insurance
Corporation
(FDIC)

The FDIC regulates banking and insures deposits up to $100,000. Its Web site has sections for consumers, bankers, analysts, and investors. It gives information on deposit insurance, consumer protection, banking trends, laws and regulations, and more.

EDITOR'S CHOICE

Access this Web site from http://www.myreportlinks.com

institution can take back physical property and then sell it to recover its losses.

Today, many people use credit to purchase goods that lose their value over time. One example is an automobile. This loss of value is called depreciation. Lenders can usually recover at least part of the value of these types of loans.

People also use credit to purchase consumable goods such as food, clothing, and entertainment. These types of purchases have little or no value that the lender can take back if the borrower does not pay. This type of credit is called consumer credit.

The independent government agencies that are mentioned in this section work primarily with investment credit. That is because when used properly, investment credit builds wealth. This increase in wealth helps create a stronger economy. On the flip side, consumer credit actually decreases wealth. The interest paid on consumer debt is for past purchases that have little or no present value.

➔OWNING PROPERTY

The American Dream—owning a home—is one way to build wealth. The Federal Housing Finance Board helps make the American Dream possible. It makes sure that local lenders have money to loan to those wanting to buy houses.

Another way for a person to build wealth is to own a business. Businesses that grow crops and raise animals for food rely on an independent government agency called the Farm Credit Administration (FCA). Many farmers and ranchers use the Farm Credit System for their financial needs. The Farm Credit System is a nationwide network of borrower-owned financial institutions that provides credit to farmers, ranchers, and agricultural and rural utility cooperatives. The FCA regulates and examines these financial institutions, ensuring compliance with the Farm Credit Act of 1971.

Credit unions, too, are borrower-owned and operated. To join a credit union, a person must

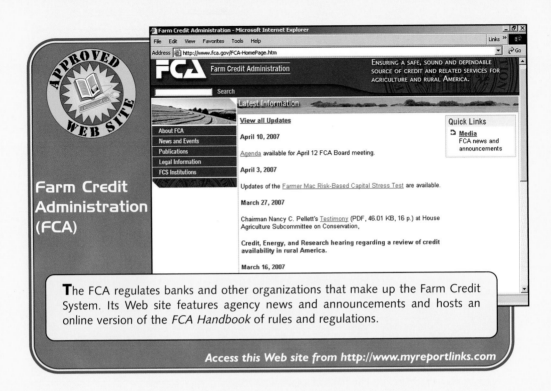

Farm Credit Administration (FCA)

The FCA regulates banks and other organizations that make up the Farm Credit System. Its Web site features agency news and announcements and hosts an online version of the *FCA Handbook* of rules and regulations.

Access this Web site from http://www.myreportlinks.com

first be a member of the participating organization. The National Credit Union Administration (NCUA) charters and supervises federal credit unions. It also insures the savings in all federal and most state-owned credit unions. Credit unions offer a full variety of credit, not just investment loans.

One last independent agency related to credit is the Export-Import Bank of the United States (Ex-Im Bank). This bank works with businesses from other countries that want to buy United States goods or services, but who are not able to pay for the goods up front. Ex-Im Bank finances the purchases of United States goods. This helps the American businesses grow and helps keep the United States economy strong.

⊖RETIREMENT SAVINGS

One reason people want to generate wealth is to be able to live well in retirement after they stop working. If a person spends all of his income as he makes it during his employable years, then he will have nothing left to live on after he stops working. The government has created several independent government agencies to help ensure that each person has some type of income when he or she retires. The money from these programs alone is rarely enough to fund a complete retirement, but they provide an easy way to begin saving.

The best known of these is the Social Security Administration (SSA). Each person who works is required to have a social security card. The SSA gives each applicant a unique, nine-digit number that becomes his or her identification number within the federal government system. Each person who works supplies this number to an employer. The employer then takes a percentage of the employee's wages and gives it to the government to hold until that person reaches retirement age. While being held, the money collects interest and grows a little over time.

The money accumulated is the property of the individual. If the person dies, the money goes to his or her survivor, called survivor benefits. If the person becomes disabled and is no longer able to work, the money is paid back to that person in disability payments starting at the time of the disability instead of during retirement.

A similar agency is the Railroad Retirement Board. This board looks after and distributes money put into retirement funds by railroad workers. These workers only pay into this fund, not into the Social Security System. The board performs the same functions as the Social Security Administration, but only for railroad workers.

Today most people who work for private companies can participate in what is called a 401(k)

With sections on Social Security, retirement planning, Medicare, disability, and more, the SSA's Web site is geared primarily to helping Americans make use of their benefits. It also features news bulletins and the agency's views on the future of Social Security.

Access this Web site from http://www.myreportlinks.com

plan, named after the part of the Internal Revenue Code that created it. In a 401(k) plan, employers collect a portion of their employees salaries and hold it for them in a tax-deferred account. Tax-deferred means that the money will not be taxed until it is distributed to its owner.

Employees choose how much they want to save of their salaries, up to a government-defined amount in a given year. Employers collect the money out of each paycheck, and then send it to an investment firm that manages the plan to increase the funds. The money is held until retirement age, and then paid out over time. The money can be removed early, but only with stiff penalties. The employer holding the money decides the penalties.

The Federal Retirement Thrift Investment Board administers a similar retirement plan for federal employees. The Thrift Savings Plan allows employees to save for retirement through a government plan.

⊜PENSIONS

Pensions are another type of account used by some employers to give people an income during retirement. A pension is a series of payments made to a person after retirement, as promised by an employer. The money for the pension comes from the employer, and must be maintained according to government regulations. The Pension Benefit Guaranty Corporation (PBGC) guarantees that pensions promised will be paid. Each pension plan pays a fee, much like an insurance premium, to the Pension Benefit Guaranty Corporation. In return, the PBGC guarantees the basic benefits of the pension plans.

CITIZEN SUPPORT

6

Although the federal government spends a lot of its resources helping businesses succeed, it also helps its citizens. The government seeks to protect an individual's freedoms and quality of life. It promotes a sense of community and national pride. It cares about individuals.

➡ EQUAL RIGHTS

Dr. Martin Luther King, Jr.'s, famous "I Have a Dream" speech, delivered on August 28, 1963, set hearts on fire. Up until that point, King had led and participated in nonviolent protests against discrimination and unfair laws of the Southern states. These laws, known as the Jim Crow laws,

Martin Luther King, Jr., led the famous "March on Washington" on August 28, 1963.

mandated that blacks and whites have separate facilities in public places. King used these protests to draw attention to the lack of basic civil rights for blacks. Blacks did not have the right to vote, were segregated from whites in public places such as restrooms and buses, had separate schools with far less acceptable facilities, and did not have an equal chance at job opportunities or at higher education.

EQUAL EMPLOYMENT

King was instrumental in gathering popular and political support for the civil rights of African Americans and other minorities in the United States. President John F. Kennedy introduced legislation for what became the Civil Rights Act of 1964, but was assassinated before it became law. However, Kennedy did sign an executive order creating the Equal Employment Opportunity Commission (EEOC). The EEOC serves as the legal enforcement for equal opportunity in employment. It can bring a lawsuit against a private employer on behalf of an employee. It also adjudicates for claims of discrimination brought against federal agencies.

The U.S. Commission on Civil Rights, a separate independent agency, functions as a sort of watchdog. It investigates complaints of civil rights violations, but it primarily collects information related to discrimination, analyzes it, and then reports on it to the government and the public.

→EQUAL OPPORTUNITY

Another agency that functions along similar lines is the National Council on Disability (NCD). Its primary goal is to ensure a high quality of life for those citizens with disabilities. NCD's stated purpose is "to promote policies, programs, practices, and procedures that guarantee equal opportunity for all individuals with disabilities, regardless of the nature or severity of the disability; and to empower individuals with disabilities to achieve economic self-sufficiency, independent living,

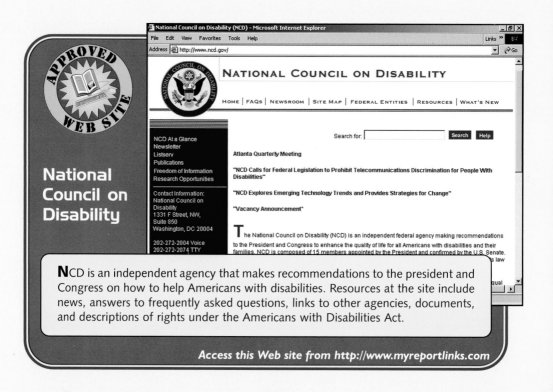

NCD is an independent agency that makes recommendations to the president and Congress on how to help Americans with disabilities. Resources at the site include news, answers to frequently asked questions, links to other agencies, documents, and descriptions of rights under the Americans with Disabilities Act.

Access this Web site from http://www.myreportlinks.com

and inclusion and integration into all aspects of society."[1]

On a very practical level, the NCD has worked to make sure that government and other public buildings provide access to the handicapped. This includes things like wheelchair ramps, wider doorways, and handicapped restroom facilities.

→COMMUNITY SERVICE

Every community has needs that have to be met. Every citizen has something to contribute to his or her fellow humans. The Corporation for National and Community Service helps bring these two together so each person can help out his or her local community.

The Corporation for National and Community Service's job is to promote citizenship, service, and responsibility. It provides opportunities for Americans of all ages and backgrounds to serve their communities through three organizations: Senior Corps, AmeriCorps, and Learn and Serve America.

Senior Corps works to engage the people with the most life experience in volunteering their time and wisdom. Senior Corps works with people over fifty-five to help them become mentors, coaches, or companions to people in need, or to contribute their job skills and expertise to community projects and organizations. Learn and Serve connects

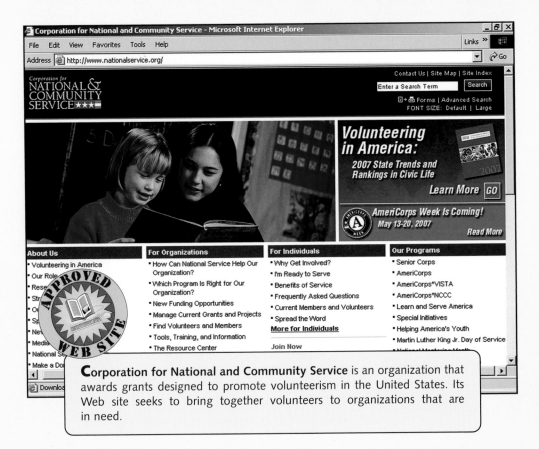

Corporation for National and Community Service - Microsoft Internet Explorer

File   Edit   View   Favorites   Tools   Help   Links »

Address http://www.nationalservice.org/   Go

Contact Us | Site Map | Site Index

Corporation for
NATIONAL &
COMMUNITY
SERVICE ★★★ ▀

Enter a Search Term   Search

→ Forms | Advanced Search
FONT SIZE: Default | Large

**Volunteering
in America:**
2007 State Trends and
Rankings in Civic Life
Learn More GO

AmeriCorps Week Is Coming!
May 13-20, 2007
Read More

About Us
• Volunteering in America
• Our Role
• Rese
• Str
• O
• Sp
• Ne
• Media
• National S
• Make a Do

For Organizations
• How Can National Service Help Our
  Organization?
• Which Program Is Right for Our
  Organization?
• New Funding Opportunities
• Manage Current Grants and Projects
• Find Volunteers and Members
• Tools, Training, and Information
• The Resource Center

For Individuals
• Why Get Involved?
• I'm Ready to Serve
• Benefits of Service
• Frequently Asked Questions
• Current Members and Volunteers
• Spread the Word
More for Individuals

Join Now

Our Programs
• Senior Corps
• AmeriCorps
• AmeriCorps*VISTA
• AmeriCorps*NCCC
• Learn and Serve America
• Special Initiatives
• Helping America's Youth
• Martin Luther King Jr. Day of Service
• National Mentoring Month

Download

Corporation for National and Community Service is an organization that
awards grants designed to promote volunteerism in the United States. Its
Web site seeks to bring together volunteers to organizations that are
in need.

community service with classroom learning for
students of all ages.

AmeriCorps is a network of local, state, and
national service programs that connects volunteers to needs in education, public safety, health,
and the environment. Volunteers may work with
public agencies or not-for-profit, faith-based, or
community organizations. Service opportunities
include things like tutoring and mentoring disad-
vantaged youth, building affordable housing,
helping communities respond to disasters, and
other vital tasks.

Individuals who volunteer benefit in a variety of ways. They receive personal satisfaction from helping others and develop character as they work with others toward a common goal. A volunteer may be able to build skills in an area not open to her in the job market. Full-time participants can

▲ *These Girl Scouts worked with the Corporation for National and Community Service in Fairfax, Virginia, to deliver kits to less fortunate people in their county. They donated their time to aid in community outreach on Martin Luther King, Jr., Day.*

earn money toward college. Both volunteers and their communities win.

→HELPING INDIVIDUALS

"What will I do when I get out? I don't have a home. I have no job skills. The only life I know is the one I came in here with." These could be the words of any person coming out of prison who wants to live a decent life, but is having trouble getting back into society.

While the Corporation for National and Community Service helps whole communities, the Court Services and Offender Supervision Agency (CSOSA) for the District of Columbia helps individuals. The people helped are those being released from jail. When an offender is released, he often has no home, no job, and few real life skills to help him cope with leading a "normal" life. CSOSA helps offenders rejoin their communities. It provides life-skills training, substance abuse treatment, job training and housing assistance, sex offender registration, and other vital programs.

CSOSA uses the McGruff the Crime Dog program to work with the children of offenders. Kids can learn about safety and how not to become victims of crime. CSOSA also provides support in the area of parenting.

GOVERNMENT SUPPORT

7

Over the years, several independent government agencies have been set up to support the government itself. Some of these manage government land, facilities, and employees. Others ensure elections are fair. Still others make sure the main branches of the government are properly following procedures and operating with high standards.

→ELECTIONS

One of the greatest freedoms in America is the freedom to vote. The United States government is designed to be representative of the people. Its main job is to support its citizens and protect their freedoms.

President Clinton gives his second inaugural address after being sworn into office on January 20, 1997. The monitoring of elections is a key task of some independent agencies.

In general, it is assumed that United States citizens are a self-governing people. This right of self-government is the foundation of the U.S. Constitution. The Constitution guarantees each individual's freedoms, yet allows the government to act in the people's behalf.

The principle of self-government assumes that individuals will try to follow the laws of the land and will work toward the good of their local communities. In turn, their leaders will act for the common good of all people, not in the spirit of self-interest or the good of only a few. Americans are allowed to vote for the leaders who will govern their lives. These elected officials are honor-bound to represent the wishes of the people who put them in office.

Fair elections are key to this representative form of government. Unfortunately, it is expensive to run for office. It takes thousands of dollars to get the word out about a candidate's views and voting record. Some candidates may have access to more money than others. They may be able to afford to buy radio and television ads that their opponents cannot afford.

⊖FEDERAL ELECTION COMMISSION

The Federal Election Commission (FEC) was created in 1975. The FEC enforces the Federal Election Campaign Act. This act places limits and

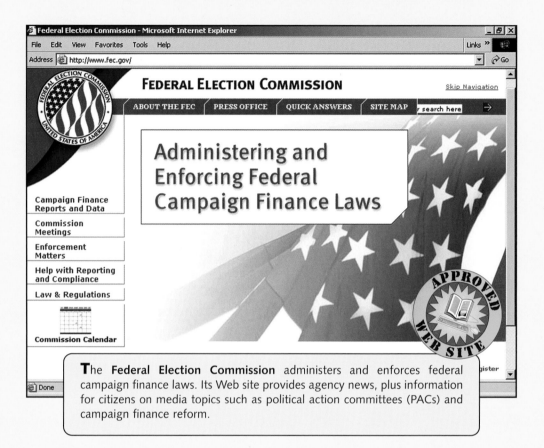

The **Federal Election Commission** administers and enforces federal campaign finance laws. Its Web site provides agency news, plus information for citizens on media topics such as political action committees (PACs) and campaign finance reform.

prohibitions on certain types of campaign donations. It also requires candidates of federal elections to reveal how much they spend on their campaigns. One other function is to oversee the public funding of presidential elections.

The 2000 presidential election was surrounded by controversy. State after state, the tallies came in. As the numbers mounted, neither candidate—Al Gore nor George W. Bush—showed a clear margin for victory. It came down to the results in one state: Florida. The number of ballots cast for the candidates was so close that ballots had to be recounted to make sure the numbers were correct. The recounting process brought to light a problem with the voting process. Most counties in Florida used a punch card system rather than computerized voting machines. If the punch card machines were not used properly, the card would have an incomplete punch. The race was so close that these partially punched cards became a big deal. They were such a big deal that there was no winner declared in the presidential race that year until thirty-five days after the election.

To avoid this and similar problems in the future, the Election Assistance Commission (EAC) was created in the Help America Vote Act of 2002. Its first responsibility is to provide funds to states to replace their punch card systems. Beyond that, the EAC helps states to administer federal elections by reviewing existing processes and procedures in order to avoid problems like the one in 2000.

⊜GOVERNMENT LAND, FACILITIES, AND PERSONNEL

The executive branch of the federal government functions like a business. It runs the day-to-day operations of the United States. There are three independent agencies that manage many of the

Pierre L'Enfant was chosen to develop what has become the National Mall in Washington, D.C. The National Mall is the home of many of the country's most beautiful monuments such as the Lincoln Memorial, Vietnam War Memorial, and Washington Monument.

government's property and employees.

The first of these, the National Capital Planning Commission, works with federal land in and around the capital city, Washington, D.C. The city of Washington, D.C., was planned in 1791 by Pierre L'Enfant, a friend of George Washington. L'Enfant developed a plan that featured ceremonial spaces and grand avenues, while respecting the natural landscape. The result was a system of intersecting diagonal avenues superimposed over a grid system. The avenues radiated from the two most significant building sites that were to be occupied by houses for Congress and the president.

Two hundred years since its design, L'Enfant's plan—with its landscaped parks, wide avenues, and open space allowing intended vistas—is still intact. The National Capital Planning Commission continues to keep L'Enfant's vision alive. It works to preserve the beauty and historic design of the federal land around the Capitol. It also protects and enhances the historical, cultural, and natural resources in the District of Columbia, northern Virginia, and Maryland where federal land and buildings are located.

➡ THE GENERAL SERVICES ADMINISTRATION

The second agency for property management, the General Services Administration (GSA), manages all the facilities of the federal government. It supports federal employees wherever they work. This could be in an office building, a warehouse, a national forest, or out of a government car. GSA provides workspace, security, furniture, equipment, supplies, tools, computers, and telephones. GSA also provides travel and transportation services, oversees telecommuting centers and federal childcare centers, and evaluates government-wide policies. In 2000, GSA created FirstGov.gov (now USA.gov), the United States government's official Web portal.

The third agency, the Office of Personnel Management (OPM), manages the people side of the business. It is the federal government's human resources (HR) department. It functions much like private sector HR departments. It sets government pay scales by geographic region and

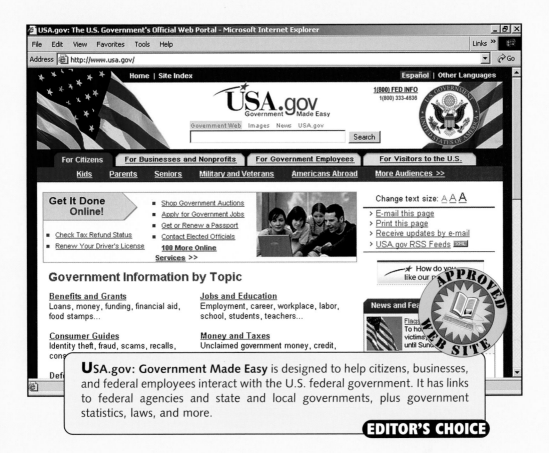

USA.gov: Government Made Easy is designed to help citizens, businesses, and federal employees interact with the U.S. federal government. It has links to federal agencies and state and local governments, plus government statistics, laws, and more.

EDITOR'S CHOICE

ensures the government uses fair hiring practices. The OPM administers the government's benefits program, and maintains employee records.

These last two agencies keep the government running smoothly. GSA helps keep costs down by consolidating purchasing contracts to get the best deal. OPM sets standards to ensure that government employment practices are consistent throughout the federal government, regardless of location.

→ACCOUNTABILITY

Accountability means accepting responsibility for your actions. One reason the United States government works so effectively is its built-in accountability among the three branches: the executive, the legislative, and the judicial. In addition to the built-in system of checks and balances related to power, there are independent government agencies that monitor the ethical practices of our leaders.

→SAFETY AND PROTECTION

The Office of Compliance administers and enforces the Congressional Accountability Act. The act applies eleven existing employment, civil rights, health, and safety-related statutes and regulations to the legislative branch. For the executive branch, there is the U.S. Office of Government Ethics. It is tasked with establishing standards of conduct and setting conflict of interest policies.

The Office of Special Counsel (OSC) investigates allegations of prohibited personnel practices (PPPs). In particular, it protects federal government whistle-blowers. A whistle-blower is an employee who reports wrongdoing by his or her employer. OSC becomes the legal team for those who have been wrongfully or illegally treated. OSC works either directly with the offender or through the U.S. Merit Systems Protection Board, another independent government agency.

The United States Merit Systems Protection Board protects federal merit systems for employees against abuses by agency management. A merit system is the system through which employees are rewarded or punished for behavior and performance at work. The board primarily rules on complaints about suspensions, demotions, and furloughs; violations of the various acts that govern the rights of federal employees; and management decisions that affect employee benefits.

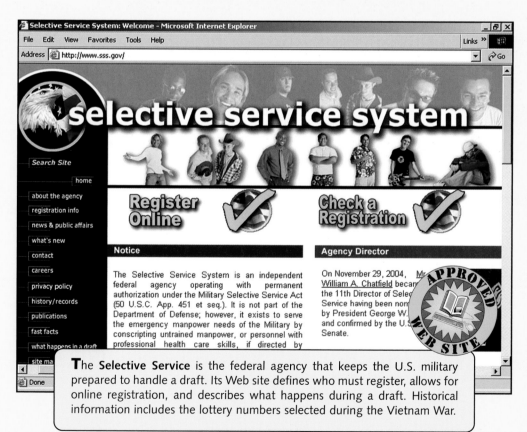

The **Selective Service** is the federal agency that keeps the U.S. military prepared to handle a draft. Its Web site defines who must register, allows for online registration, and describes what happens during a draft. Historical information includes the lottery numbers selected during the Vietnam War.

It receives allegations from OSC and hands down decisions.

→ MILITARY

Today, every United States soldier is a volunteer. United States citizens are not required to serve in the military. However, young men ages eighteen to twenty-five are required to register with the Selective Service. This registration provides a record of potential soldiers in the event of a war.

The Selective Service System was started in 1940 as a peacetime draft. It operated from 1948 until 1973 to fill vacancies in the military. During that time, young men were called into mandatory service in the military. The draft was suspended in 1973, but the Selective Service registration requirement was reinstated in 1980. Although only registration is required today, the mandatory requirement to join the military could be reinstated by Congress at any time for emergency military needs.

→ HISTORICAL DOCUMENTS

At the time of the War of 1812, many important historical documents were stored in the White House. As British soldiers neared Washington, D.C., President James Madison joined in the fight. His wife, Dolley Madison, stayed behind. They agreed to meet at a particular place if the redcoats should make it all the way into the District of Columbia.

On the evening of August 24, 1814, the drums of the British forces could be heard advancing on the city. Dolley Madison knew she must flee. As she was being whisked away by guards, she

▲ As the British Army was burning Washington, D.C., during the War of 1812, First Lady Dolley Madison courageously saved a portrait of George Washington and other famous documents.

realized that several items valuable to the young American nation were left in the house. Against the pleas of her bodyguards, she ran back into the house. She gathered the famous full-length painting of George Washington and some important documents. Popular myth tells of her heroic attempt to save the original copy of the Declaration of Independence, but that had been moved earlier and was safely stored in Leesburg, Virginia.[1] Dolley made it out of the house just as the redcoats arrived. They destroyed the White House and everything that she had left behind. If not for her quick thinking and absolute bravery, Charles Willson Peale's now-famous portrait of George Washington and the other documents would have been lost forever.

NATIONAL ARCHIVES

The nation's most important documents are now safely stored in the National Archives Building in Washington, D.C. There is a second storage facility located in College Park, Maryland. The nation's archives are overseen by the National Archives and Records Administration (NARA). NARA is charged with preserving and maintaining crucial government and historical records. The National Archives contain original copies of the Constitution, the Bill of Rights, the Louisiana Purchase, and the Emancipation Proclamation.

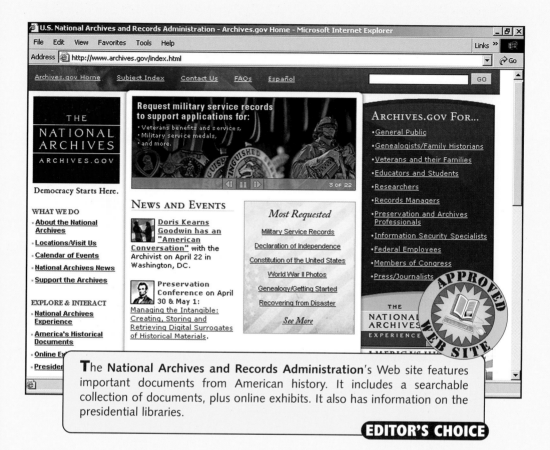

APPROVED WEB SITE

The **National Archives and Records Administration**'s Web site features important documents from American history. It includes a searchable collection of documents, plus online exhibits. It also has information on the presidential libraries.

EDITOR'S CHOICE

NARA also maintains the Office of Presidential Libraries. It has eleven presidential libraries and the Nixon Presidential Materials. The presidential libraries are like a cross between an archive and a museum. They contain all the documents and artifacts of a president and his administration. For example, if the president receives a gift from the leader of another country on an official visit, that artifact would end up in his presidential library. It is not really the president's personal property. According to the Presidential Records Act of 1978, it belongs to the people of the United States.

8 COMMUNICATION AND TRAVEL

Every time you listen to the radio, watch television, or use your cell phone, the government has been involved. Every time you send or receive mail through the post office, you have encountered an independent government agency.

COMMUNICATION

Control of communication lines is of great importance in the Information Age. The Federal Communications Commission (FCC) is an independent government agency directly responsible to Congress. It regulates interstate and international communications by radio, television, wire, satellite, and cable. The FCC's area of authority

This modern communications tower includes both TV and radio antennae. An independent agency is responsible for monitoring what goes over U.S. airwaves.

covers the fifty states, the District of Columbia, and United States possessions.

To accomplish the task of managing such a wide array of communications, the FCC is divided into six bureaus and ten staff offices. In general, the staff offices support the work of the bureaus. The bureaus and staff offices work together to accomplish the goals and orders of the FCC.

For example, the Media Bureau regulates both AM and FM radio. It also regulates all types of television: broadcast stations, cable television, and satellite services. One of the things it regulates is what type of programming content is considered decent or indecent. This debate has been in the news quite a bit. Many groups have different ideas about what is decent. The Enforcement Bureau is in charge of enforcing the decency standards for radio and TV. When there is a complaint about what is considered decent, the Office of Administrative Law judges would get involved. A television or radio station can be fined if it broadcasts content the FCC finds to have been indecent.

➔WIRELESS

The growth of wireless communications has exploded with the use of cell phones, pagers, wireless Internet, and two-way radios for emergency responders. The Wireless Telecommunications Bureau oversees and regulates these areas and the types of devices that use radio waves to communicate.

Radio waves travel in a limited range of frequencies. These frequencies are divided up and assigned to users by the Office of Engineering and Technology. The FCC limits the operating ability of each radio station within a certain frequency and power range. When you press the 'seek' button on your car radio, it searches through all FCC-approved radio frequencies to find stations broadcasting in your area.

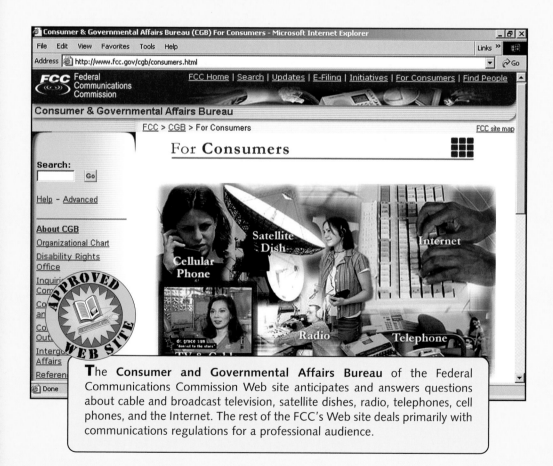

The **Consumer and Governmental Affairs Bureau** of the Federal Communications Commission Web site anticipates and answers questions about cable and broadcast television, satellite dishes, radio, telephones, cell phones, and the Internet. The rest of the FCC's Web site deals primarily with communications regulations for a professional audience.

The availability of radio frequencies has become a big issue in the communications industry. Frequencies were first assigned to radio, then television, and then cellular phone companies. Now, cable companies and telephone companies are vying for their own frequencies in the competition to offer wireless Internet service. The FCC will have to sort this out by gathering information and analyzing data. Eventually, the FCC will assign bandwidth according to use and the market will have to adjust.

→ BROADCASTING

On the international side, the International Broadcasting Bureau (IBB) maintains United States government-funded, nonmilitary broadcast services. These services include Voice of America (VOA), Radio Sawa, and Radio and TV Marti (Office of Cuba Broadcasting). It also provides support to Radio Free Europe/Radio Liberty and Radio Free Asia.

Voice of America was launched in 1942. Today, it broadcasts one thousand hours of shows a week and reaches an estimated 100 million people. One program it airs is *America's Global College Forum.* The host of this show interviews students from around the world who are studying in the United States. Another program, titled *American Stories,* is simply readings of short stories. You can listen to Voice of America and other programs of the IBB through the Internet.

⊜AMTRAK

In the early days of the twentieth century, long-distance travel was best accomplished by train. By the 1940s, more and more people owned automobiles, roads were becoming better, and air travel was becoming more popular. Train travel became the slower and less convenient means of long-distance travel. Independent passenger train

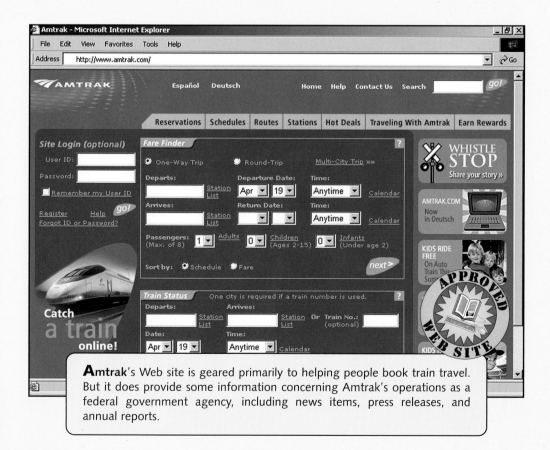

Amtrak's Web site is geared primarily to helping people book train travel. But it does provide some information concerning Amtrak's operations as a federal government agency, including news items, press releases, and annual reports.

services suffered from competition, bad service, and run-down accommodations.

In 1970, in an effort to revive passenger rail service, Congress passed into law the Rail Passenger Service Act. The act created the National Railroad Passenger Corporation, with the business name Amtrak. Amtrak was a coming together of several of the existing passenger train services. It became a nationwide passenger rail service, operating as a private corporation with government backing.

Passenger train service is not one of the most popular modes of travel today. However, it may yet see a revival. Gas prices continue to climb and air travel is increasingly inconvenient due to security measures. Another practical reason is simply space. Highly populated and urban areas may not be able to support additional roads or airports to handle an increase in traffic. Amtrak continues to look toward the future to meet the challenge of the nation's transportation needs.

→UNITED STATES MAIL

You have received mail. You may have even been to the post office. But how much do you really know about the post office? Check your knowledge against these questions:

- •What organization is the third largest employer in the United States?

- Who owns the largest fleet of privately owned vehicles?
- What two postal systems are operated jointly by the USPS and the Department of Defense?
- What is a stamp collector called?
- What is the requirement for having your picture on a stamp?

The answer to the first two questions is the United States Postal Service (USPS). The postal

▲ *This letter sorter carries out an important task at one of the United States Post Office terminals. Letter sorters go through thousands of pieces of mail per day so that it can all get delivered to the correct address.*

service handles 800 billion pieces of mail every year. When a person mails a letter, it usually goes through one or more processing centers before arriving at its destination. Some letters are sent using tracking information such as registered mail, certified mail, and express mail. The post office posts the tracking info online as it travels through the various mail centers. Here is a typical day in the life of a postal carrier from San Antonio, Texas.

A Day at the Post Office

Upon arrival, the letter carrier checks in and immediately gives her vehicle a safety inspection. Then, she collects her scanner for tracking any mail that is registered or needs a signature. Almost all mail goes through a processing center and is scanned there, but some mail arrives at the station that the processing center did not have time to scan and sort. The letter carrier hand scans and hand sorts this mail, called "casing it." The post office also employs mail handlers. The mail handlers will sort the oversize mail and parcels, then put them on gurneys for the letter carriers.

The letter carrier adds her presorted mail and cased mail to the gurney, and then loads her vehicle. On the way out, she makes three more stops. First, she stops by the Mark Up box and tosses in any mail that has been sorted wrongly, badly

The USPS Web site is mostly functional, providing businesses and consumers with postal rates, zip-code lookup, etc. It also has postal news, stamps for sale, and information on service to the community.

Access this Web site from http://www.myreportlinks.com

addressed, or is otherwise not deliverable. Next stop is the Hot Case to check for any last minute mail, some of which may have come from yesterday's Mark Up box. The last stop is with the accountable clerk. This person processes any mail items that the post office is responsible for, such as those needing signatures. If a letter needs a signature and no one is at home to sign for it, the letter carrier leaves a note giving the addressee several options on what to do. Both the undelivered letter and the note when it is returned go to the accountable clerk. When the addressee requests another try at delivery, the accountable clerk gets it ready.

Once the truck is loaded, the letter carrier delivers the mail. Mail routes are determined by approximately how long it will take to deliver. Each piece of mail has a time to deliver assigned to it. Based on the typical volume of sorted mail and the number of packages that day, the letter carrier estimates the time it will take to deliver and applies for any overtime before she even leaves the station. Once the time request is approved, she is on her way.

On question three, many people might know at least one of the answers if they have sent mail

▲ Before a letter or package can be sent it must have the proper postage. The amount of postage can vary depending on the size and weight of the package and how soon the sender would like it to be delivered. This box is marked with priority postage.

to people in the military. The USPS and the Department of Defense jointly operate the Army Post Office (APO) for the Army and Air Force, and the Fleet Post Office (FPO) for the Navy, Marine Corps, and Coast Guard.

All mail must have postage. First-class mail, postcards, and parcel post packages require a postage stamp or a metered stamp. The USPS issues new postage stamps each year. People who collect stamps are called philatelists. A philatelist would know that only a person who has been dead for at least ten years can be featured on stamps. Presidents are the only exception to this rule. A president can be honored on a stamp beginning with the first anniversary of his death.

The USPS does not set its own postage rates. There is a second independent government agency, the Postal Regulatory Commission, which determines how much it will cost to send the various classes of mail. The Postal Regulatory Commission reviews changes in postal rates and fees requested by the Postal Service. This review process ensures that the USPS raises rates in a fair and necessary manner.

9 SCIENCE, THE ARTS, AND HUMANITY

Although not part of the everyday operations of the government, science and the arts are important to a society. The quality of these two areas is an indication of the quality of the society that produces them. How a society values humanity—especially humanity outside of its own borders—is another mark of quality. Several independent government agencies have been created to promote these three areas: science, the arts, and humanity.

→SCIENCE

The Space Race began in 1957 with the Soviet Union's launch of *Sputnik I*, the first man-made satellite. As *Sputnik* circled Earth, it could be seen in the October sky. Homer Hickam, Jr., a high school student in a West Virginia mining town saw *Sputnik* pass by. He decided right then that he wanted to build rockets. *October Sky,* the movie based on Hickam's attempts to build rockets, captures the excitement of catching up to the Russians in space exploration.[1] Hickam dreams of getting out of that coal-mining town and working for the National Aeronautics and Space Administration (NASA).

NASA

NASA was created in 1958, just a few months after the Soviet Union's launch of *Sputnik.* NASA's purpose was to counter the perceived threat of the Soviet Union's superior technology. NASA launched a series of successful projects during its first years. Each project was a stepping-stone to the next one. The *Mercury* program, which ran from 1961 to 1963, tested sending a single astronaut into space to see if he could survive. The honor of First American in Space goes to Alan B. Shepard, Jr., for his fifteen-minute ride in a *Mercury* space capsule in 1961. In 1962, John Glenn, Jr., became the first United States astronaut to orbit Earth. Three years later, Edward H. White, Jr., conducted the first spacewalk by a United States astronaut as part of the *Gemini* project.

NASA's greatest achievement during these early years was sending man to the moon. The *Apollo* program included seventeen spaceflights. The early missions were used to test things like orbiting the moon. These flights provided

information for *Apollo*'s ultimate goal: putting man on the moon. On July 20, 1969, Neil A. Armstrong became the first of only twelve astronauts to walk on the moon. As he stepped onto the moon, he uttered his famous words, "One small step for man. One giant leap for mankind." NASA had proved its superiority over the Soviets.

NASA went on to produce *Skylab,* an orbiting workshop where astronauts stayed in space for up to eighty-four days. Then came the Space Shuttle program, which still operates. The most recent large-scale space project is the International Space Station (ISS). It is a joint effort among the United States, Russia,

Alan Shepard was the first American to go into space. Here, Shepard is being lifted out of the ocean after landing back home on Earth.

Japan, Canada, and some Euro-
pean nations. It is ironic that
what began as a furious competition between the United States
and Russia (once a part of the
Soviet Union) is now a friendly
partnership.

In addition to these manned
projects, NASA launches communications and weather satellites.
It also sends unmanned probes
out into the far reaches of the
solar system. Probes have landed
on Mars, and flown past Saturn
and Jupiter. NASA works on
other projects, too. Its research
on wind shears, aerodynamics,
and rocket design has been
applied to planes such as the
F/A-18 Hornet and the Boeing
777. NASA continues to research
designs of high-speed aircraft.

In the movie *October Sky*,
Hickam and his three friends

Neil Armstrong took this picture of fellow ▷
astronaut Buzz Aldrin as Aldrin walked on
the Moon.

finally do figure out how to build and launch rockets. They enter their project in local, regional, and then national science fairs. These science fairs were an outgrowth of the government's new focus on science. In 1950, Congress created the National Science Foundation (NSF). Its purpose was "to promote the progress of science; to advance the national health, prosperity, and welfare; to secure the national defense . . ."[2]

FOCUS OF THE NFS

Today, the NSF funds about 20 percent of all federally supported basic research conducted by America's colleges and universities. It is the only federal agency whose mission includes support for all fields of fundamental science and engineering, except for medical sciences. The NSF works in a variety of fields from astronomy to geology to zoology. It does not operate its own laboratories, but instead issues grants for research. The NSF tends to keep its focus on research that is fully integrated with education. By doing this, projects and research in educational institutions train future engineers and scientists.

Hickam and his friends go on to win first place in the national science fair. Hickam accepts a scholarship to Virginia Tech and eventually goes to work for NASA. Although he never realizes his

National Aeronautics and Space Administration

+ Text Only Site
+ Non-Flash Version
+ en Español
+ Site Help & Preferences

FIND IT @ NASA :

+ GO

+ Advanced Search

+ ABOUT NASA   + LATEST NEWS   + MULTIMEDIA   + MISSIONS   + MY NASA   + WORK FOR NASA

+ For Kids
+ For Students
+ For Educators
+ For Media & Press
+ For Researchers
+ For Industry
+ For Employees

TO THE MOON AND BEYOND:
BUILDING THE VISION FOR SPACE EXPLORATION

+ LIFE ON EARTH   + HUMANS IN SPACE   + EXPLORING THE UNIVERSE

04.11.07
AIM Set to Study Polar Clouds
+ AIM Page

04.10.07
Earthquakes May Quickly

04.17.07
Expedition 15 Takes Charge After Ceremony
+ Space Station Section
+ Boston Marathon Video

04.17.07

04.18.0
Astro
Planet
+ Read

04.13.07
Report Reve

The **National Aeronautics and Space Administration's** massive Web site spotlights the agency's history, current missions, space research, and technology. Pictures, audio, and video from NASA spaceflights are included, as are links to subagencies and information on careers.

EDITOR'S CHOICE

dream of going into space, he becomes a trainer of space shuttle crews.

→THE ARTS

Libraries and museums help their patrons experience the world. Museums collect historical items and information that help us understand long ago and faraway places as well as the world around us. Libraries hold vast amounts of information about almost any topic and provide starting points for scholarly research. The Institute of Museum and Library Services provides leadership and funding for the nation's libraries and museums. Its vision for these institutions is clear:

> As stewards of cultural heritage, information and ideas, museums and libraries have traditionally played a vital role in helping us experience, explore, discover and make sense of the world. That role is now more essential than ever. Through building technological infrastructure and strengthening community relationships, libraries and museums can offer the public unprecedented access and expertise in transforming information overload into knowledge.[3]

➲ LIBRARIES

This last point is key. Finding information is easy. Finding reliable information takes work. Although Internet research is convenient, it is sometimes difficult to verify the accuracy and reliability of its sources. Librarians and museum curators offer years of training in research using scholarly sources. For example, your librarian can direct you to books in the library to suit your needs. But your library card gives you access to hundreds of electronic databases through the library's Web site. You can find databases of articles from newspapers, periodicals, and scholarly journals. You can find literary criticism, written at the time the author published the work, as well as modern criticism reflecting how views of a particular work have

On October 2, 2007, the National Endowment for the Arts named its Jazz Masters for 2008. Pictured here from left to right are NEA Chairman Dana Gioia, and jazz greats Tom McIntosh, Candido Camero, Joe Wilder, and Gunther Schuler.

changed over time. Librarians can point you in the right direction for your research.

National Endowment for the Arts (NEA) is another independent government agency, created to promote art in the culture. Its mission is "supporting excellence in the arts, both new and established; bringing the arts to all Americans; and providing leadership in arts education."[4] Because American art is a reflection of our history

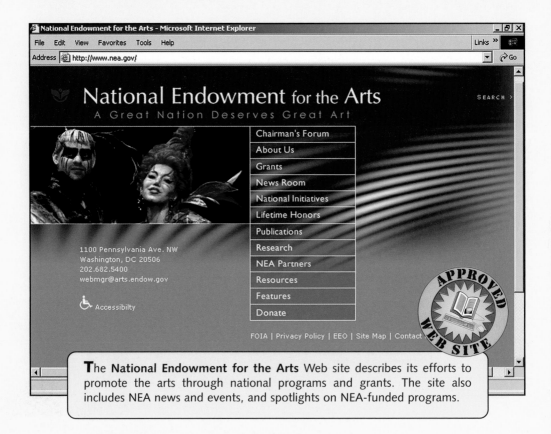

The **National Endowment for the Arts** Web site describes its efforts to promote the arts through national programs and grants. The site also includes NEA news and events, and spotlights on NEA-funded programs.

and our heritage, it is important to support artists who hold up the mirror for us.

Moving beyond appreciation of United States art and culture, the National Endowment for the Humanities (NEH) was established to promote knowledge of human history, thought, and culture. This includes the study of cultures of any time period or from any land. NEH awards grants to help create and preserve knowledge, identify and promote reliable learning resources, and empower teachers through offering professional development programs.

→HUMANITY

The federal government has a stake in helping other countries. Its reasons are threefold: humanitarian, economic, and political. As one of the richest nations on Earth, the United States is in a good position to help other countries in need. Some of its efforts are strictly to relieve suffering. This type of aid is called humanitarian aid.

The second reason for helping other countries is economic. When countries develop a healthy economy, the people become consumers. Consumerism creates jobs in the developing country and creates a potential place for businesses in the United States to sell goods. This helps businesses in the United States expand and grow.

The third reason is political. Helping others gives the United States a chance to influence those countries toward a democratic form of government. A free market economy thrives in a democratic society, one where the government lets the demands of the market drive the economy. When people experience the benefits of economic success, it fuels the drive to continue that success through a government that will support it.

The United States government has created several independent government agencies specifically to help other countries with their economic development. The Inter-American Foundation (IAF) works with organizations in Latin America

The **Peace Corps** tries to promote international understanding through volunteerism. Its Web site describes its mission, history, and current operations. It tells what it is like to volunteer for the Peace Corps, and has resources for teachers, students, and previous volunteers.

and the Caribbean. It gives money to local interests that are working to improve the quality of life of people in need. To qualify, part of this improvement must include strengthening participation in the local government, accountability to the supporting organization, and promotion of democratic practices.

The Peace Corps is another agency designed to promote the United States' interest in promoting democracy, especially in developing countries. It was founded in 1961 to counter the threat of the spread of communism. At the time, the Soviet Union and China were seeking inroads into Third World countries to promote a communist form of government. The Peace Corps operates with three goals:

- Helping the people of interested countries in meeting their need for trained men and women.
- Helping promote a better understanding of Americans on the part of the peoples served.
- Helping promote a better understanding of other peoples on the part of Americans.[5]

When a country requests aid, Peace Corps members are matched with the needs.

➡ IMPROVING DEVELOPMENT ABROAD

The African Development Foundation (ADF) works just with the people of Africa. Its mission is to help Africans participate in the economic and social development of their countries. ADF provides small grants of $250,000 or less to independent African businesspeople, small businesses, and producer associations. These groups must be working to stimulate the local economy, improve the livelihoods for those in rural areas, and assist in the development of their countries.

The United States Agency for International Development (USAID) is another organization that offers nonmilitary foreign aid. USAID receives overall foreign policy guidance from the State

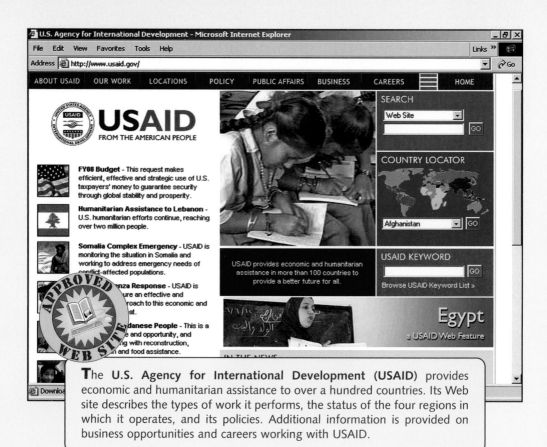

U.S. Agency for International Development - Microsoft Internet Explorer

File Edit View Favorites Tools Help   Links »

Address 🔗 http://www.usaid.gov/   ▼ 𝒫 Go

ABOUT USAID   OUR WORK   LOCATIONS   POLICY   PUBLIC AFFAIRS   BUSINESS   CAREERS   ≡   HOME

USAID
FROM THE AMERICAN PEOPLE

FY08 Budget - This request makes efficient, effective and strategic use of U.S. taxpayers' money to guarantee security through global stability and prosperity.

Humanitarian Assistance to Lebanon - U.S. humanitarian efforts continue, reaching over two million people.

Somalia Complex Emergency - USAID is monitoring the situation in Somalia and working to address emergency needs of conflict-affected populations.

...nza Response - USAID is ...ure an effective and ...roach to this economic and ...at.

...danese People - This is a ...e and opportunity, and ...g with reconstruction, ...n and food assistance.

USAID provides economic and humanitarian assistance in more than 100 countries to provide a better future for all.

SEARCH
Web Site ▼
GO

COUNTRY LOCATOR
Afghanistan ▼ GO

USAID KEYWORD
GO
Browse USAID Keyword List »

Egypt
a USAID Web Feature

The **U.S. Agency for International Development (USAID)** provides economic and humanitarian assistance to over a hundred countries. Its Web site describes the types of work it performs, the status of the four regions in which it operates, and its policies. Additional information is provided on business opportunities and careers working with USAID.

Department. It advances United States foreign policy by supporting economic growth, global health, and democracy. It works to prevent conflicts and give humanitarian assistance. USAID operates in four regions of the world: Sub-Saharan Africa, Asia and the Near East, Latin America and the Caribbean, and Europe and Eurasia.

➔ BY THE PEOPLE, FOR THE PEOPLE

Although each independent government agency performs different functions and meets different needs, each stands for one purpose: to serve the overall and individual interests of the people of the United States. Some of these agencies touch almost every aspect of our lives; others we may never need. Some serve us; others give us opportunities to serve. Either way, each one is a monument to our uniquely democratic form of government—a government by the people, for the people.

Report Links

The Internet sites described below can be accessed at http://www.myreportlinks.com

▶**National Archives and Records Administration**
Editor's Choice Get in touch with U.S. history at the National Archives.

▶**National Aeronautics and Space Administration**
Editor's Choice Learn about the operations and history of the nation's space agency.

▶**LSU Libraries Federal Agencies Directory**
Editor's Choice Here is a good starting point for doing further research on government agencies.

▶**U.S. Environmental Protection Agency**
Editor's Choice Learn about the EPA and how it works to protect the environment.

▶**USA.gov: Government Made Easy**
Editor's Choice Get it done. Interact with your government.

▶**Federal Deposit Insurance Corporation (FDIC)**
Editor's Choice See how the FDIC helps keep the banking system stable in the United States.

▶**Amtrak**
Learn about the operations of Amtrak, the nation's railway.

▶**CIA: *The World Factbook***
The Central Intelligence Agency has prepared info on the nations of the world.

▶**Consumer and Governmental Affairs Bureau**
This Web site helps answer consumer questions about TV, radio, telephones, and the Internet.

▶**Corporation for National and Community Service**
See how you can make a difference. Learn about volunteering in your community.

▶**Farm Credit Administration (FCA)**
Learn how the Farm Credit Administration helps support farmers in the United States.

▶**Federal Election Commission**
Learn about the FEC's role in elections and campaign finance.

▶**National Council on Disability**
Learn about the agency supporting federal efforts to help Americans with disabilities.

▶**National Endowment for the Arts**
Learn about the operations of the federal agency devoted to supporting the arts in the United States.

▶**National Labor Relations Board**
The NLRB helps workers and employers maintain a good relationship.

Report Links

The Internet sites described below can be accessed at
 http://www.myreportlinks.com

▶**National Transportation Safety Board**
Learn about traffic safety and regulation.

▶**Occupational Safety and Health Administration (OSHA)**
Workplace safety is important. Here's where you can learn all about it.

▶**Overseas Private Investment Corporation (OPIC)**
Read about a government agency that supports American investment to promote free markets.

▶**Peace Corps**
Find out what it is like to volunteer for the Peace Corps.

▶**Selective Service**
Information about the federal agency that administers wartime drafts.

▶**Social Security Online**
Learn about retirement planning and benefits through the nation's entitlement programs.

▶**United States Coast Guard**
Research the Coast Guard's missions and history.

▶**United States Nuclear Regulatory Commission**
Read about the agency that regulates nuclear power and nuclear waste in the United States.

▶**United States Postal Service**
See how the United States Postal Service serves the community through its Web site.

▶**United States Trade and Development Agency**
Read about a federal agency that helps promote economic development in foreign nations.

▶**U.S. Agency for International Development (USAID)**
Learn about the economic and humanitarian aid programs run by USAID.

▶**U.S. Consumer Product Safety Commission**
The Consumer Product Safety Commission aims to keep Americans safe.

▶**U.S. Equal Employment Opportunity Commission (EEOC)**
Learn about protection from discrimination on the job at the Web site of the EEOC.

▶**U.S. Securities and Exchange Commission**
The SEC oversees the trading of stocks.

▶**U.S. Small Business Administration**
See how the Small Business Administration helps Americans get a business up and running.

Cabinet—A group of important individuals selected by the president to help him run the executive branch. They are usually colleagues whose advice and views he respects and trusts.

civilian—A person who is not a police officer, firefighter, or is serving in the armed services.

Cold War—A period that lasted from 1947 to about 1991 in which the United States and the Soviet Union engaged in a struggle for power. It was not a declared military war, but a race to be the superpower of the world.

commission—A group or organization that is given the authority to carry out the wishes of others. These groups have the power to make laws and decisions.

Congress—The legislative branch of the United States government. Congress decides on which laws are passed that will govern the nation. The House of Representatives and the Senate make up the two houses of Congress.

Department of Commerce—The Cabinet department of the U.S. federal government that promotes economic growth.

Department of Energy—The Cabinet department of the U.S. federal government that is in charge of the country's energy policy and nuclear safety.

Department of Homeland Security—The Cabinet department of the U.S. federal government that is in charge of protecting the country's territory from attacks by terrorists. Commonly referred to as Homeland Security, this department also is responsible for taking action when natural disasters occur.

Department of Labor—The Cabinet department of the U.S. federal government that oversees the workplace. It sets health and safety standards that all businesses are to respect and follow.

Department of Transportation—The Cabinet department of the U.S. federal government that is responsible for ensuring a national transportation system that is safe, fast, accessible, and convenient. This system includes railroad, highway, and aviation transport.

executive branch—The part of government that enforces the laws. This branch handles all of the day-to-day operations. The president holds this office and is helped by a staff.

executive order—An order given by the president that is as powerful as if it were the law.

federal government—The central government of a country. The U.S. federal government is divided into three main branches—executive, legislative, and judicial.

free market—A system of buying and selling that is not controlled. No one has the power to tell you what you purchase or sell.

furlough—When an employee is given a furlough, it means he or she has been allowed a temporary leave of absence from his or her job.

Information Age—Period estimated to have begun in the early 1970s when the movement of information became faster than physical movement. The telephone, cell phone, Internet, and fax machine are all contributors to this movement.

intelligence—Information that is collected and studied about an enemy or a potential threat. This information may be about a foreign government, their military, corporations, or individuals.

interstate commerce—Business done between two or more states.

judicial branch—The part of government that is made up of all the courts. They listen to and judge cases brought before them that challenge laws that have been passed by Congress and signed by the president. The Supreme Court is the highest court.

jurisdiction—The power and permission to read and understand the law as you wish and make your decisions based on how you have interpreted it. When someone has jurisdiction, he or she basically has the powers of a judge.

KGB—The name of the police organization of Russia when it was a Soviet (Communist) country. It was their spy force. In English the initials stand for State Security Committee.

legislative branch—The part of government that makes the laws.

private sector—The part of the business world that is not controlled by the state or federal government.

State Department—Also known at the U.S. Department of State, this agency is in charge of all foreign affairs for the United States. Among other duties, it works to protect Americans living or traveling abroad, to assist U.S. companies that do business with other countries, and to keep the American public informed about relations with other nations.

Third World—This term refers to countries that are considered the poorest and least developed in the world. Today the term is considered offensive and nations considered to have a low standard of living are referred to as "developing" or "underdeveloped."

Treasury Department—"Treasury" refers to the place where the treasure is stored. This department of the U.S. federal government is where all of the country's money is kept and managed. Among other duties, it is in charge of collecting taxes, managing the government's bills and expenses, and producing new coinage.

union—An organized group that stands up for the workers. Union members, under the guidance of chosen leaders, negotiate with management to make sure workers are treated fairly on the job, that they receive decent pay, and that they have good working conditions.

Chapter 1. The EPA Called Into Action

1. Hard Aground: Disaster in Prince William Sound," *Anchorage Daily News,* March 24, 1989, <http://www.adn.com /evos/pgs/intro.html> (January 26, 2007).

2. Ibid.

3. Traci Watson, "The End of an Arctic Paradise," *USA Today,* n.d., <http://www.jomiller.com/exxonvaldez/usatoday4.html> (January 26, 2007).

4. Ibid.

Chapter 3. Safety and Security

1. "CPSC Overview," *U.S. Consumer Product Safety Commission,* n.d., <http://www.cpsc.gov/about/about.html> (January 26, 2007).

Chapter 4. Commerce and Business

1. Jose's Hermie Hut is not an actual business. Any resemblance to real or fictional people or situations is strictly coincidental.

2. Fictional Web site.

Chapter 5. Financial

1. Alan Greenspan, "Commencement address, At the Wharton School, University of Pennsylvania, Philadelphia, Pennsylvania," *The Federal Reserve Board,* May 15, 2005, <http://www .federalreserve.gov/boarddocs/speeches/2005/20050515/> (January 26, 2007).

Chapter 6. Citizen Support

1. *National Council on Disability,* n.d., <http://www.ncd .gov/> (January 26, 2007).

Chapter 7. Government Support

1. Anthony S. Pitch, "The Burning of Washington," *The White House Historical Association,* n.d., <http://www.whitehousehistory .org/08/subs/08_b04.html> (January 26, 2007).

Chapter 9. Science, the Arts, and Humanity

1. October Sky, directed by Joe Johnston, Universal Pictures, 1999.

2. "About the National Science Foundation," *National Science Foundation,* n.d., <http://www.nsf.gov/about/> (January 26, 2007).

3. "About Us," *Institute of Museum and Library Services,* n.d., <http://www.imls.gov/about/about.shtm> (January 26, 2007).

4. "About Us," *National Endowment for the Arts,* n.d., <http://www.arts.gov/about/index.html> (January 26, 2007).

5. Peace Corps, "What is the Peace Corps?" *About the Peace Corps,* n.d., <http://www.peacecorps.gov/index.cfm?shell =Learn.whatispc.mission> (October 2, 2007).

Binns, Tristan Boyer. *The CIA: Central Intelligence Agency.* Chicago: Heinemann Library, 2003.

————. *The EPA: Environmental Protection Agency.* Chicago: Heinemann Library, 2003.

Fuller, Donna Jo. *The Stock Market: How Economics Works.* Lerner Publishing Group, 2005.

Friedman, Mark. *Government: How Local, State, and Federal Government Works.* Mankato, Minn.: The Child's World, Inc., 2004.

Harmon, Daniel E. *The Environmental Protection Agency.* Philadelphia: Chelsea House Publishers, 2002.

Horn, Geoffrey M. *Cabinet and Federal Agencies.* Milwaukee: Gareth Stevens Audio, 2003.

Mello, Tara Baukus. *The Central Intelligence Agency.* Philadelphia: Chelsea House Publishers, 2000.

Spangenburg, Ray, and Kit Moser. *The History of NASA.* New York: Franklin Watts, 2000.

Stein, R. Conrad. *The National Archives.* New York: Franklin Watts, 2003.

Suen, Anastasia. *The Peace Corps (Reading Power: Helping Organizations).* New York: PowerKids Press, 2002.

WITHDRAWN